HARD YEARS:
ANTIDOTES TO AUTHORITARIANS

EUGENE J. MCCARTHY

HARD YEARS:
Antidotes To Authoritarians
by
Eugene J. McCarthy

© 2000 by Eugene J. McCarthy
ISBN 1-883477-38-7
Library of Congress CIP 99-068859

Published by LONE OAK PRESS

Cover photo courtesy
National Oceanic & Atmospheric Administration

Contents

Foreword by Richard Broderick

In reading <u>Hard Years</u> I was reminded of an unusual fact about the book's unconventional author: Besides being an important political figure, Eugene McCarthy is a poet, and an accomplished one at that.

Evidence for this pops up throughout these pages, and not just in obvious places, such as in his poem "Ares" or his verse praising Robert Lowell. Take, for example, his description of Lyndon Johnson's attitude toward Congress, and the way it builds upon an initial trope to divert us into a much more multivalent comparison.

"He [Johnson] had experience in driving cattle, where the technique is to start the cattle slowly and then stampede them at the end. But when you deal with Congress, you should know about the psychology of pigs, which is opposite that of cattle. In driving hogs, you start them as fast as you can, you make all kinds of noise, and you try to panic them. You shout at them in Latin. But once they are started, you slow them as you go along. When you get them right up to the pen you want them in, you come to a stop. The pigs will then look right and left and think that they have discovered it. And in they go."

In addition to mild surprise at discovering that such an urbane and witty man appears to know a lot about pigs (and setting aside an obvious resemblance here to Lincoln's homespun humor) there are several things about this passage that deserve further examination.

By unpacking McCarthy's second image, we find that it looks in several different directions. Incorporating into itself the popular cliché of politicians as pigs at a trough, it reaches forward toward a more complex understanding of group motivation while also turning back on itself, or at least on its author who was himself a senator during the Johnson years, and therefore one of the "hogs." This, in turn, lends an affectionate rather than merely acerbic tone to the imagery. Ultimately what the passage encodes is evidence of a mind at play, treating the most serious topics - including an awareness of its own limitations - with a ludic spirit rare in any walk of life, but virtually unheard of in the self-regarding, hyperbolic world of electoral politics. An attentive reader is led to the inescapable conclusion that these words, and others like them throughout Hard Years are the product of a first-rate poetic sensibility as well those of a first-rank political thinker. Is it any surprise that the man who wrote this book should later go on to publish a sometimes hilarious, sometimes touching collection of political beasts?

Passages of wit, perspicuity, charm, insights both oblique and arresting, a tone of voice that might be termed "laconic ebullience," abound in Hard Years. At the same time there is something very republican (small r) about McCarthy's penchant for understatement, his insistence on the primacy of reason, his careful restatement of the indispensability of checks and balances. As a poet, McCarthy is an ironist - a stance borne of a mature and realistic apprehension of existence. As a politician and political thinker, that maturity and realism leads him again and again to remind us that the government established by the Founding Fathers is not so much a system designed to exercise as to limit government power. In this regard it's important to remember that his early, unfailingly principled opposition to the Vietnam War was fueled in equal measure by his rejection of overreaching Presidential powers (and American imperial ambition) and his moral repugnance at the war's brutality and futility.

Above all, Hard Years creates the indelible impression of a man of great integrity, whose responses to the world are of a piece, with values, beliefs, behavior, and native temperament wholly consistent with each other. By book's close, we are left with a sense of McCarthy as a figure who has more in common with the authors of the Constitution and The Federalist Papers than with any contemporary American politician.

In the end, Eugene McCarthy's contribution to the history of the past 50 years could be described in the words he himself employs in the posthumous tribute to John F. Kennedy that appears in the section entitled "A Good Person Is Not So Hard To Find."

"What should be remembered," McCarthy says of his fellow Irish-American politician, "is the promise and the style... For he brought to that office a willingness to accept with good heart the burden and responsibility of citizenship. He brought the spirit of public happiness which possessed the American colonists at the time of the Revolution and which was reflected in their delight in public discussion and public action, in joy of citizenship and civic commitment, in self-government, in self-discipline in a political community."

The years covered in this book were indeed hard years. But throughout, they were leavened, even, in part, redeemed - as this book serves to remind us - by the political courage, philosophical cogency, moral integrity, and restrained though poetic eloquence of Eugene McCarthy.

October 10th, 2000

Introduction by Tom Wicker

Gentlemen that day abed may not think themselves accurs'd nor hold their manhoods cheap whilst any speaks who hauled voters to the polls for Gene McCarthy on March 12, 1968. Still, it was a kind of Saint Crispin's day in American politics, and not just because McCarthy managed to wrest forty per cent of the vote and most of the delegates away from President Lyndon Johnson in the New Hampshire primary.

This book is not about that primary, or the McCarthy campaign of 1968, or more than partially about politics. It was written over a span of roughly six years; but because these writings, among other things, reflect McCarthy's political ideas, which were so often unorthodox but prescient when first spoken, it does convey something of the flavor of those remarkable times when he was setting loose new forces in American politics as few before and none since have done.

McCarthy's presidential campaign, legitimated that snowbound day in New Hampshire, was important in itself. It exposed Johnson's weakness, demonstrated the political potential of the antiwar movement, and brought Robert Kennedy belatedly into the presidential race. All this, together with the developing certainty of a McCarthy victory in the Wisconsin primary, forced Johnson's withdrawal, which made possible the beginnings of peace negotiations in Paris. If none of that had happened, neither Richard Nixon nor Hubert Humphrey, the ultimate candidates that year, might have gone as far as he did in pledging to end the war in Vietnam. And it now seems clear that had Humphrey been only marginally more willing at the Democratic convention to make concessions to the McCarthy-Kennedy forces - which by 1972 came to dominate the party under the banner of George McGovern - and their point of view about the war, Humphrey would have been elected in November, instead of Nixon with his tiny 43.4 to 42.7 per cent plurality.

But to look at the McCarthy campaign only in the context of 1968 is to miss its real importance, which lay in the longer-term development of American politics.

Probably no other loser in American history had a more profound impact. For example, George Wallace, a loser that same year, had strong implicit influence on Nixon's later policies, just as Adlai Stevenson, losing in 1952 and 1956, still had much to do with the style and personnel of the Kennedy administration a few years later.

Gene McCarthy's campaign had that kind of residual influence, too; those who supported him were prominent among those who achieved the Democratic presidential nomination for George McGovern four years later, as well as the far-reaching reforms that overhauled the party processes in 1972 and for 1976. But McCarthy's real impact was on politics itself, not just on his party.

For one thing, his willingness to challenge Johnson, who had seemed unchallengeable, and his promise to change Johnson's war policy, which had seemed unchangeable, electrified American youth, evoked their idealism and energy, and brought them into party and elective politics to a degree that far surpassed McCarthy's stated intention to appeal to them, or anybody's expectations.

One minor but telling example: in Indiana, precinct voter lists were compiled alphabetically rather than by street addresses. This made block-by-block canvassing unnecessarily difficult, but Indiana's old-line "pros" had been making do with the system for years. A few young zealots for McCarthy, reared in the computer age, cadged some free computer time on a machine at Indiana University and converted the alphabetical lists into street-address lists. The so-called pros, not for the last time in the presence of a new generation, were dumbstruck at the canvassing that resulted. And surely McCarthy's various campaign headquarters were the first ever to feature child-care areas, where volunteer mothers could leave their children to play while they put in long hours for the McCarthy campaign.

The McCarthy campaign was not, of course, the only factor in the massive influx of youth into elective politics from 1968 onward; it was just the first and probably the main influence. Moreover, the activism and performance of young people in 1968, for McCarthy and later for Robert Kennedy, surely speeded the day of the eighteen year-old vote, the full importance of which will not be known for years to come.

It is true enough that the antiwar movement of the sixties produced the McCarthy campaign, rather than the other way round; but antiwar leaders had to look long and hard for a politician willing to go along with them. Without McCarthy to take the antiwar movement into party competition and party primaries, to give it a workable political potential, far more of the youth segment of the movement might well have gone the way of the Students for a Democratic Society (SDS), into the futility and violence of the Weathermen. And the campus violence, upheaval, and alienation that was so widespread in 1969 and 1970 might well have been much worse had there not been some evidence from 1968 that American politics could produce a man willing to stand up, and voters willing to back him.

Besides, McCarthy made the campaign more than an antiwar effort. For it was not just young people and opponents of the war that flocked to the McCarthy standard. He appealed mightily also to intellectuals, independents, the educated, to public-spirited citizens turned off by politics-as-usual, the war, Lyndon Johnson, big government, failed promises, and bureaucratic bungling. McCarthy appeared personally to be their kind of man: witty, urbane, one who read books and poetry and could even write them, eloquent but not windy, bold enough to bypass the usual political pretensions and pomposities, intelligent enough to think for himself, independent enough to say what he thought.

Those qualities appealed to voters old enough to remember them in Adlai Stevenson - and who had thought they spied them in John Kennedy. But the McCarthy campaign was more than stylish; erratic and jerry-built as it often was, it had a substantive intellectual content that not even Stevenson, certainly not Kennedy, perhaps no presidential candidate since Woodrow Wilson, had dared put before an American public that most politicians seemed to consider mired forever in the cliches of the New Deal, World War II, and the Cold War.

Eugene McCarthy was the first serious presidential candidate of modern times who challenged American institutions and processes rather than praising them - the first candidate, Arthur Schlesinger, Jr., quipped at the time, to run for President against the powers of the presidency. He was exactly that, and it does not seem so incongruous after Watergate - nor did it at the time to millions of McCarthy supporters and antiwar voters fed up with the high hand of Lyndon Johnson. Eventually, Schlesinger, never the possessor of a closed mind, came to write a book called The Imperial Presidency - an institution that McCarthy had done much to identify.

McCarthy, however, undertook to "demythologize" the presidency at a time when Franklin D. Roosevelt and Harry S. Truman had made its occupant a sort of universal "Commander in Chief," Eisenhower had made him a national father figure, Kennedy had turned his prominence into high glamour, and Johnson had made him the whole world's range boss, crisis manager, and button-masher. Asked what he would do if he became President, McCarthy first said he would "go to the Pentagon"; later he said he would take down the fence around the White House.

More seriously, he consistently made the point reiterated in this volume: "For effective government in the twentieth century, the presidency must first of all be depersonalized. We do not need Presidents who are bigger than the country, but rather ones who will speak for it and support it. The disposition to look upon the presidency as a splendid misery or a monarchy must be revised ... We must return to the founding fathers' concept of the presidency as an office of significant but limited power. It must again be an office that shares both power and responsibility with the other branches of government and with the people." To say such things in 1968 was to stand against virtually the entire body of political-science thought since the advent of FDR

On the eve of the Democratic convention, when McCarthy still might have had a chance to be nominated, the Warsaw Pact powers invaded Czechoslovakia and put an end to the "Prague spring." It chanced that McCarthy had a Washington news conference scheduled for the next day, and when it was convened, the reporters demanded to know what, as President, he would have done about events in Eastern Europe.

Nothing, McCarthy replied, in a few unexcited words to that effect.

Astounded, the reporters demanded to know why he would have done nothing, against every tradition of the imperial presidency.

Because, McCarthy replied calmly, there's nothing I could have done.

He went on to suggest that the lights that had burned late in the White House the night before, the agitated comings and goings of L.B.J. and his cohorts, were mostly window dressing. Johnson was not going to do anything either, could do nothing, but was making a great show of doing something anyway - managing the crisis, firing off cables, phoning up bureaucrats, solemnly briefing senators. When all that was finished, McCarthy observed, the Prague spring still would be over and the Warsaw powers still would be in charge in Czechoslovakia - as they were, a subsequent fact which failed to dispel the outrage and disdain of reporters used to imperial bluster and occasional imperial action from every President back to Harry S. Truman.

That kind of candor can look like ignorance or callousness or worse, which is why most politicians do not indulge in it. McCarthy paid dearly for the fact that his plainspeak did not appeal to all voters in 1968. But the placid reaction of the nation to the denouement in Southeast Asia seven years later suggests that what was heresy then is more or less commonplace today - witness also the War Powers Act and the failure of Congress to be stampeded into throwing good aid after bad in the closing days of the Vietnamese and Cambodian wars. McCarthy was far ahead of his time in recognizing and saying that a presidency swollen with unchecked power had thrown the entire American political system out of its essential balance.

Nowhere was that more true than in foreign policy, which had become as institutionalized as the imperial presidency. When the Senate Foreign Relations Committee was told that a declaration of war on North Vietnam was not needed, that Lyndon Johnson's Tonkin Gulf Resolution was the "functional equivalent" of such a declaration, McCarthy abruptly left the hearing room.

"This is the wildest testimony I ever heard," he told reporters. "There is only one thing to do - take it to the country."

No one else thought that even that would do much good, but McCarthy did take it to the country - and not just the question of Vietnam. In his primary foreign-policy speech, he said in words that seem the more remarkable when it is remembered that they were spoken in early 1968: "America in the period of the fifties and sixties built up for itself a mission in which we were to take upon ourselves the duty to judge the political systems of other nations - nearly all the nations of the world - accepting that we had the right to interfere with all of those systems if we found them to be wanting. We spoke with great flourish of making the world safe for diversity, while in fact we were denying and even destroying diversity when it failed to meet our specifications and our standards.

"We put little confidence in diversity in Latin America unless that diversity acknowledged the authority of the United States of America or our position. Diversity in Southeastern Asia became a positive obstacle to American purposes."

Thus, he said, Washington became "the world's judge and the world's policeman," acting upon such assumptions as "America's moral mission in the world; the great threat from China; the theory of monolithic Communist conspiracy; the susceptibility of political problems to military solutions; the duty to impose American idealism upon foreign cultures, especially in Asia."

And the crucial point was that "gradually these assumptions, built into institutions, became more or less articles of faith and tended to escape any kind of examination or any kind of accountability to national politics or to the people of this country."

The interacting debacles of Vietnam and Watergate, the successive disasters of Lyndon Johnson and Richard Nixon, finally wrecked those articles of foreign policy faith and reduced the imperial presidency to something commensurate with the American system. But the McCarthy campaign first called serious political attention to what was wrong, first demonstrated the presence of serious political dissent from the prevailing faith, first shook those underlying assumptions for many who would later drop or modify them. Such "accountability" as may have been reestablished began with Eugene McCarthy's challenge to Lyndon Johnson in the New Hampshire primary of 1968.

"Accountability" - for institutions as well as men - is an idea that recurs throughout this book. In 1968 it was a main theme of the McCarthy campaign (again, remarkably; in 1964, after all, L.B.J. had won his landslide with the question, "Whose finger do you want on the button?" - scarcely a reminder of the democratic process or the consent of the governed). McCarthy had been, for instance, an early congressional critic of the

Central Intelligence Agency. In the 1968 campaign he was the first presidential candidate to raise the question whether this secret empire was accountable even to the government, let alone to the people. Everybody questions the CIA now.

McCarthy's ideas about "accountability" were aptly illustrated in his call for the dismissal of J. Edgar Hoover - perhaps the gravest heresy and the most prescient act of the 1968 campaign. Repeatedly, McCarthy said about what he said in Portland, Oregon, on May 27 - that as President he would fire Hoover because "everybody knows that in a formal sense the FBI is subject to the Attorney General, but you allow someone to be built up like J. Edgar Hoover - it's as though he's not to be challenged." So two things could be done: "The first is to change the whole agency, and there's no need for that. As I see it, the other is to really remove from office the person in whom that kind of what seems to be independent authority has developed."

Hoover, whose reappointment had been John Kennedy's first act as President and whose exemption from normal retirement at age seventy had been procured by Lyndon Johnson, promptly demonstrated his arrogance by distorting this out of all proportion: "All Americans," he wrote in the FBI Law Enforcement Bulletin, "should view with serious concern the announced intentions and threats by a political candidate, if elected, to take over and revamp the FBI to suit his own personal whims and wishes." Only after Hoover's death did it become clear to all whose personal whims and wishes had been running the FBI all along.

McCarthy also attacked the Pentagon and the accepted American reliance upon military strength for leverage in the world, as well as an imperial foreign policy. He frankly stated his "moral opposition" to the war in Vietnam when others complained only that it couldn't be won. He abandoned both the hortatory personal style Americans had become accustomed to in politicians and the interest-group basetouching that had been regarded as elementary in politics. Blacks and the poor got so little special attention as to turn off many of them and shock more conventional liberals. The District of Columbia delegation, heavily black, found him so cool that when he told them to go look up his record, a black delegate burst out: "Record, hell! Tell us what you feel."

All this had its effect, or at least its reflection, on politics, too, and not altogether happily. Moralism pervades politics today on issues far less fundamental than Vietnam, and it is generally believed now that liberal Democratic politics became too closely identified with the black movement in the sixties, greatly facilitating the resurrection of Richard Nixon and the rise of George Wallace. But in 1968 McCarthy's broad assault on what were then the taboos of American politics, at a time of overwhelming institutions, unreachable government, and unstoppable war, had the effect of making him look like one man against the juggernaut, the inner-directed and outspoken free man that everyone wishes to be, at least in the heart.

He still appears that way in this book. Here are not only the well-remembered McCarthy attitudes, once so unorthodox, now become conventional wisdom, and the corrosive McCarthy wit ("When Mr. Nixon proposed an Eleventh Commandment during the 1972 campaign, the time had come for everyone to manifest concern about the power of the presidency"), but the gift for the telling comparison ("At times, the Senate seems to be the last primitive society. It has great respect for seniority, which is of primitive disposition. It has great respect for occupancy and for the territorial imperative; you can scarcely move a senator out of an office, even after he has died. And the Senate has its own trial by ordeal, which is called the filibuster").

Here, too, is the persistently off-angle way of looking at things. Who among our politicians but Eugene McCarthy would seriously put forward the proposition, strongly argued in this volume, that nonlawyers are needed on the Supreme Court ("There is need for more than a knowledge of legal precedents and procedures ... that a judge is 'thinking as a lawyer' or 'speaking as a lawyer' is not a reassuring statement when the subject matter is human rights in an age of nuclear biology").

McCarthy the writer retains the keen eye of McCarthy the politician for the essence of things ("The CIA may deserve special study as a potentially pure and perfect, self-contained bureaucracy - responsible only to itself and for itself") and the wide range of interests that marked his 1968 campaign (diffuse and disjointed, the political writers said). One finds, for example, a disquisition on "Poetry and War" followed by a poem on war by Eugene

McCarthy and that followed, not surprisingly, by a lengthy reflection on intellectuals in politics which ringingly reaffirms an old-fashioned "confidence in reason as the one truly human instrument that we must use for guidance and direction as we continue to live on the edge of disaster."

Here, too, are the harsh political judgments McCarthy was never reluctant to make (though not always of himself) - for example, of the McGovern convention victory in 1972, already cited as an outgrowth of his own 1968 campaign: "Whereas those who controlled in 1972 were more sophisticated and less physical than those who ran the 1968 convention, their methods were essentially the same. When the party rules were more useful than the law, the rules were applied, as in the rejection of Mayor Daley's delegation. When the law was advantageous, as in the issue of sharing the California delegation, the law was applied. So the defeat of 1972 was not at all surprising."

McCarthy here ponders, as always, questions of values ("...technical progress, in a sense uncontrolled and not subject to truly rational direction, threatens to become the source of values in itself ...") and responsibility ("We have a right to say to the corporations, 'We have given you special privileges, and here is what has happened: not enough production, not enough employment, twenty three million poor' ").

Always, he is concerned with America as a concept - with what its place and legacy as a world leader should be, not merely that it should have such a place and such a legacy. They should not result from mere military power, he asserts in words too seldom heard even in an era of so-called detente, "but by demonstrating that all of those things which we claim for ourselves - the right to life, liberty, and the pursuit of happiness and a basic belief in the dignity and worth of the individual - are the real strengths of America and that these are the best gifts we can offer to the rest of the world."

In its essence, that was what the McCarthy campaign of 1968 was about, and that is what this book is about, too. If that campaign was vitiated to some extent by Eugene McCarthy's personal errors and deficiencies, as well as by the forces he engaged when no one else had the courage, still it was much to expect that he could be not only the man for the hour in New Hampshire but also the man for a very different hour in Chicago. And now, across the hard years, with the ephemeral events of 1968 slipping inexorably into history and myth, the essence of the McCarthy campaign comes back to us in this book, compelling still, suggesting what might have been, the more prophetic in that so much of what then seemed daring is now the everyday stuff of politics.

One is tempted to say of Gene McCarthy, as he said of Adlai Stevenson to the Democrats of 1960: "Do not turn away from this man. Do not reject this man. Do not leave this prophet without honor in his own party." But such exhortations are not for writers of introductions nor in the long run are they effective counterbalances to perception. Eugene McCarthy's words finally must speak for themselves, and so must his political life.

May 13,1975

Preface

We in the United States long believed that we were the masters of organization and technology; that if anyone could make things work, we could - and better than anyone else.

We boasted that our economy was the most productive, that our technology was the best in our own time and the best in history. We said that our military establishment was the most powerful and most effective, our democracy the best in the world.

Somewhere in the last ten years, this mastery of technique and this story of success began to come apart. Things stopped working the way we thought they would.

After years of war, our military establishment was unable to force surrender on a small, underarmed, and technologically inferior country in Asia.

It was not only the total war machine that seemed to have problems. There were problems with particular instruments of war. The TFX airplane, later renamed the F-111, was meant to be the superplane of our military; it was to solve all problems and meet all needs of the Navy and the Air Force. We found that it had only one weakness: it did not fly very well.

American automobiles, once the pride of our mass-production industry, are regularly recalled for major repairs. And the ones that run are criticized as antisocial, anti-city, and dangerous to health because of their contribution to pollution. Not to mention their conspicuous consumption of precious fuel. The oil embargo and the energy shortage have shown the economy to be far more vulnerable to outside forces than Americans had previously realized or conceded. Millions of Americans are permanently poor. Ralph Nader and others constantly raise questions about the waste, ineffectiveness, and danger of consumer products.

Wall Street brokerage firms, supposedly at the core of free enterprise, have asked for government reinsurance. The Penn Central Railroad failed and had to be propped up by the government. The Lockheed Corporation, too, had to be bailed out by the government. And Pan American had to look for help in extremis from a foreign government.

Even our system of government, the democracy in which we have believed so strongly, does not appear to be working as it should. The Congress and the courts are under fire, and people now raise serious questions about the presidency. Voter turnout in the 1972 presidential election was the lowest in over twenty years. Reporters and pollsters found a sense of helplessness in citizens all over the land. Later a Vice President, and then a President, resigned in disgrace for the first time in our history.

The discovery that many things in America do not work came as something of a shock. It showed us - perhaps for the first time in our history - that our power is limited, and we are still assimilating that idea. This is one reason the times are difficult: we had to drop our notion of an assured national destiny before we could deal with things in a rational way. However wrenching the adjustment, Americans are now questioning not only operations but also ideas and institutions.

In the case of the Vietnam war, the country initially questioned only operations that were not working. But later it challenged the idea behind the war. Many Americans concluded that the problem was not so much faulty operations as it was a bad idea. The same process of reason is now being applied to other problems in the United States.

Welfare recipients and their defenders now talk about the rights of the poor. They insist that the poor are largely a consequence of a malfunctioning economic system rather than, as some would have it, of a disdain for the "work ethic."

Corporate managers now speak of the social responsibilities of their companies. They have been forced to respond to stockholders and others who ask pointed questions about corporate involvement in war, waste, and pollution.

Young people first, and now many of their elders, have been questioning unlimited consumption as the sure drive for economic and social progress.

The cities are now receiving some attention as communities subject to rational organization, rather than simple extensions of the family or tribe operating according to laws of nature.

Much remains to be done. But a beginning has been made, and it is reassuring to all who are concerned about the good of America.

In the midst of these hard years, it is important to continue the examination of our institutions, our operations, and our principles and to consider the example of persons who have met the challenge of our years with integrity and good will.

Institutions take many forms. They are always under threat from the barbarians, and sometimes from the intellectuals. Once an institution is abused or destroyed, dangerous powers can be unleashed, sometimes from the masses and sometimes from people in high places of power. In the play *A Man for All Seasons*, Sir Thomas More's son-in-law, Will Roper, said that he would cut down every law in England to accomplish a good end, to get the Devil. More replied, "Oh? And when the last law was down, and the Devil turned round on you - where would you hide, Roper, the laws all being flat? This country's planted thick with laws from coast to coast - man's laws, not God's - and if you cut them down - and you're just the man to do it - d'you really think you could stand upright in the winds that would blow then?"[1]

Rather than destroy our institutions, what we must do is restore their integrity, perfect them, and preserve them for the long haul.

We must guard against compromising our methods and principles because we are satisfied that our ends are good. The record of history shows that most bad things have been done by people who felt that their ends justified the methods they used.

This book, then, is an examination of institutions and methods, and of persons who have used them both well and ill.

---

[1] Robert Bolt, <u>A Man for All Seasons</u> (New York, 1962), Act 1, p. 38.

Part I: Institutions

Toward a More Responsible Presidency

For many years commentators, political scientists, party activists, and some Presidents advocated and supported what they called "a strong presidency," as being necessary to deal with our problems at home and abroad. Power was the fascinating and central word, and the assumption was that only a "powerful" President could be "effective."

Today students of the presidency are not so sure of their earlier conception of the office. They are taking a new look at it. Many now advocate limits on the power of the President and show greater respect for his sharing of power and responsibility with the Congress and other agencies of government. Among those who suggest that limits on presidential power are needed are George Reedy, who was press secretary to President Lyndon Johnson, and Arthur Schlesinger, Jr., an adviser in the administration of John Kennedy. Reedy, in his book The Twilight of the Presidency, calls the presidential office "the American monarchy"[2] and severely criticizes that concept. Schlesinger, in his recent book The Imperial Presidency, warns against that same concept of the office.

There were Presidents in our earlier history who were labeled "strong" or "weak." But "strength," when it was the mark of an administration, was related more to immediate demands, as in the case of Abraham Lincoln during the Civil War, than to a concept of the office. And it was not accompanied by the personalization of the office or by the use of the personal power of the office that has marked recent administrations.

Contemporary historians have generally characterized the Eisenhower presidency as a weak presidency and an impersonal one. It was neither. Although Dwight Eisenhower did not demonstrate leadership in proposing and carrying out new programs, he did show a negative

---

[2] George E. Reedy, The Twilight of the Presidency (New York and Cleveland, 1970), p. 3

strength. He stood his ground against direct intervention in Southeast Asia when he was urged to intervene by military and political advisers.

Eisenhower's personal mark was inaction and the delegation of power, sometimes beyond tolerable limits. Though he did little that was recommended to him in the way of aggressive action by John Foster Dulles, he did allow Dulles to go about the world signing the United States into treaties and other agreements, which carried in some cases legal obligations and also moral obligations to be faced in the future. And while the President's language was usually restrained when he talked of foreign policy, that of his Secretary of State was belligerent and provocative. Thus Dulles spoke of "massive retaliation," of "brinkmanship," of the "immorality of neutralism."

In dealing with domestic problems, Eisenhower personalized the office, again negatively, by making the presidential office less than it should have been and by passing responsibility to other officials of the government.

When Eisenhower left office, he warned the country against "the acquisition of unwarranted influence, whether sought or unsought, by the military-industrial complex," as though it were something that we were to expect in the future. In fact, under his administration in the post-Korean war period, that complex had been consolidated, entrenched, and all but institutionalized in the United States.

Personalization in the Kennedy administration was first noted principally as a matter of style in office. It was a pleasing style and one which the country accepted with relief. It was a sign of a more youthful and hopeful spirit, following the national and personal mood of retirement that had marked the Eisenhower administration. But the personalization of the office was marked by more than style. It was shown very early in the choice of Cabinet officers and other government officials. The top Cabinet officers were chosen quite without regard to party membership or identification with political issues. The President, in an unprecedented act and one quite unexpected, named his brother Attorney General.

It may be that the disposition to personalize an administration follows in some measure from the way in which the President receives the nomination of his party. In Eisenhower's case, the nomination was not given to him at his demand. Rather, he was asked to take it, apparently without any condition or qualification as to how he would conduct the office once elected. It has been said that had he been General William Sherman Eisenhower would have remarked, "If nominated I will run, and if elected I will not serve."

The party nomination was not given to Kennedy. He had to challenge the party, the party leaders, and some of the cliches of politics. In a way, he captured the nomination and the party and the presidency. The claim on the office came to be quite personal and even familial, somewhat like that exerted by a York or a Lancaster in medieval England.

The invasion of Cuba and the escalation of the United States involvement in Vietnam were not purely personal acts. They reflected a trend that was to be made clearer in the subsequent Johnson and Nixon administrations - namely, an acceptance of previous presidential policy as though it went with the office. In approving the invasion of Cuba at the Bay of Pigs, President Kennedy followed plans that had been initiated and carried forward during the Eisenhower administration. President Eisenhower had sent some eight hundred advisers to South Vietnam. President Kennedy added sixteen thousand troops, purportedly to protect the advisers. President Johnson increased the number to more than five hundred thousand, saying that he was only continuing and carrying forward an operation to which two Presidents before him had committed the country. Nixon continued the presidential war.

To make American power "more credible," President Kennedy sent more United States troops to Germany and increased the military budget above the forty-five billion dollars of the last Eisenhower year. How much of the military build-up, especially that dealing with missiles and nuclear power, was in consequence of the "missile gap" issue raised by President Kennedy as a candidate, and how much of it was in response to the Russian-American confrontation following the Bay of Pigs incident, is beyond determination. What is quite certain is that it was excessive. Dr. Jerome Wiesner, science adviser to President Kennedy, considered the strategic build-up "an unnecessary U.S. response."[3] In May 1970, before a Senate Foreign Relations subcommittee, Dr. Wiesner said:

> ... *Secretary of Defense McNamara's recommendation*[4] *at the time was for 950 new Minuteman missiles.... At the same time the Navy proposed increasing the Polaris submarine fleet to 41.... The explanation given by Secretary McNamara for his recommendation was that because the Air Force recommended 3,000 Minuteman missiles, 950 was the smallest number Congress would settle for. I believe that the failure to reach agreement on a nuclear test ban and the resumption of nuclear testing by the Soviet Union in the fall of 1961 were direct consequences of this buildup on our part.*

Whatever the primary motivation, the decision involved subjective, personal considerations.

The personalization of the office by President Johnson took a somewhat different form. He was never able to impose his style on government or even on the office of the presidency. This may be attributable to the fact that his style was too individualistic or too regional. But more likely it was the consequence of the way in which he came to power - through the vice-presidency and after the assassination of a President. Had he been chosen as a presidential candidate by his party and then elected, his administration undoubtedly would have been different.

President Johnson retained many Kennedy Cabinet members and advisers, and he continued the war in Vietnam. In the handling of both domestic and international problems, his personality became involved; institutional and even constitutional distinctions became more and more obscure. Although President Johnson as a rule appointed able and competent persons to high positions, he subsequently, all too often, used them for purposes other than those that they were supposed to serve in their appointed offices. Thus Abe Fortas, a competent lawyer and potentially a good (if not excellent)

---

[3] U.S. Senate, Committee on Foreign Relations, *Hearings before the Subcommittee on Arms Control, International Law and Organization*, 91st Congress, 2nd session (May 28, 1970), p.396.

[4] ibid.

Supreme Court Justice, was appointed to the Court, and then used as the President's lawyer and political consultant. Chief Justice Earl Warren, although not appointed to the Court by President Johnson, was called upon to head the commission that investigated the assassination of President Kennedy. That was essentially a nonjudicial proceeding. Arthur Goldberg, when he was Ambassador to the United Nations, was asked to step out of that role to help negotiate a labor dispute. The Senate was used as though it were the House of Representatives, and the House of Representatives, when it showed more support for presidential foreign policy, was treated as though it were the Senate.

The serious decline of the Democratic party that had started when Lyndon Johnson was Senate Majority Leader continued through his presidency. The National Committee was downgraded, and even the responsibility for financing party affairs and campaigns was largely shifted to Capitol Hill. Eventually the party structure became almost meaningless. It was reduced to being little more than an agent of the President rather than, as it should have remained, an agent of the people. When President Johnson announced that he would not run again for the presidency in the spring of 1968, only seven months before the November election, the treasury of the Democratic party was practically empty.

As his administration went on, President Johnson was inclined to use the possessive pronoun "my" about more and more institutions and instruments of government and politics. In a similar way, he personalized the war or at least the criticism of the war, although he justified his continuation of it as a responsibility of the presidential office. Certainly he did not stand against the pressures for escalation from the military men, who were sustained by soothsayers and prophets of success such as Dean Rusk, Robert McNamara, and Walt Rostow. President Johnson repeatedly stated that he was only carrying on the policies of previous Presidents, citing Eisenhower's aid to Diem in South Vietnam and Kennedy's commitment of American troops. Johnson ignored, or chose not to recognize, the fact that no President is absolutely bound by what his predecessors have done.

As the war in Vietnam continued to go badly, and as escalation after escalation failed to achieve the projected goals, the President moved to make the continuation of the war - and vindication of his role in perpetuating the war - the substance of the politics of 1968. He left it as a burden on the candidates of both major parties in the campaign of that year.

The process was analyzed and described by Stephen Vizinczey in an essay in his book <u>The Rules of Chaos</u>:

> ... *To withdraw from Vietnam, Johnson would have had to lose faith in, and then be willing to explode, the myth of power and thus the myth of the United States as "the most powerful nation the world has ever seen." To quit Saigon and acknowledge that the United States could not impose its will on even a small part of a tiny and primitive country would have been to demonstrate the Absurdity of Existence - the problem his experts were trying to solve with computers.*[5]

> *Besides, how could Johnson have shed the delusion of his nation, when most of his critics shared it? They told him that he should use the immense power of his office for better purposes! So this great might that everybody was talking about had to exist somewhere, it had to materialize with a few more marines, social workers, ambassadors, bombs. But while none of these could turn a single Vietnamese into a Johnson Democrat, the bombs did go off and thereby strengthened his illusion that if he could destroy the world, he must also be able to control it. So he couldn't let go. This was the psychology of escalation, the dynamic of the obsession.*

Vizinczey wrote that when President Johnson found he "would have to give up either the war or the presidency, Johnson chose the war. He let go of power altogether rather than face up to the fact that he had never had it. This is how men hang on to their obsessions: they would sooner give up a pound of flesh than an ounce of illusion..."[6]

The presidency of Richard Nixon was personalized in a different way. It was not so much possessive as incarnational. Early in his administration, Mr. Nixon

---

[5] Stephen Vizinczey, <u>The Rules of Chaos</u> (New York, 1969), p. 71.

[6] ibid., p. 72

began to use the plural "we" without specifying who was included. Mark Twain once said that no one had a right to use the indefinite "we" except the King of England, the Pope, or a person with a tapeworm. With Nixon, there was also a focus on the loneliness of the office, the retreats to Camp David, the mystique almost to the point where it took on a religious character. When Mr. Nixon proposed an Eleventh Commandment during the 1972 campaign, the time had come for everyone to manifest concern about the power of the presidency.

The first disturbing evidence of Nixon's overpersonalization of the office was his statement that the President of the United States was the moral leader of the country. Certainly that was to assert too much. President Ford came close to saying the same thing when he remarked that he would not have a code of conduct for members of his administration, but that his example would be their guide.

At the beginning of his first term, President Nixon said that he would have a strong and responsible Cabinet, suggesting that even Cabinet members' wives would be involved in administration decisions. Differences of opinion were to be respected. The first break in this facade came with the firing of the Secretary of the Interior, Walter Hickel, over a disagreement on conservation policy. More serious was the growing disposition to exclude Cabinet members from central policy-making and to transfer that role to White House aides and advisers (the inner ring directed by H. R. Haldeman and John Ehrlichman) and to transfer foreign policy responsibility from the Secretary of State to the assistant for national security affairs.

There was some justification, on the basis of the record, for conservative and even moderate Republicans to criticize the Nixon opening of relations with Mainland China and his move to further detente with Russia. Those actions contradicted established Republican positions and Nixon's own long record of opposition to any such policies.

The incarnational concept of the Nixon presidency was manifest in his approach to two other important institutions, the Supreme Court and the United Nations. He tried to change the Court so that it would reflect his own views. This conflicted with the traditional ideal that the Court should represent the best and wisest historical and judicial judgment.

Insofar as one can conclude from his appointments, Mr. Nixon viewed the office of United States Ambassador to the United Nations as simply an extension of the presidential office. There was no consideration of the special commitments of the United States under the Charter of the United Nations, nor of the ratification of that charter by the Senate of the United States. Instead of appointing established and highly reputable persons who had independent political support, he appointed a career diplomat, then a man who had been defeated as a candidate for the Senate, and finally a television correspondent.

A President can be a good President and an effective one without overpersonalizing the office or abusing the other agencies and institutions of government and without qualifying as a "strong" President according to recent definition.

Franklin D. Roosevelt was an effective national leader without being a particularly "strong" President. During his first years in office he tried to be "strong." He failed. Much of the early New Deal legislation, including the Railroad Pension Act and the Guffey-Snyder Coal Act, was thrown out by the courts. In 1935 the Supreme Court declared unconstitutional the code-making provisions of the National Industrial Recovery Act. In 1936 it found unconstitutional the processing tax of the Agricultural Adjustment Act, calling it an improper exercise of the tax power and an invasion of the rights of the states.

Roosevelt's effort to pack the Court by appointing a new justice for each justice over the age of seventy was an attempt to exercise strength. It aroused great public indignation, for however much the people might have been annoyed with Court obstructionism, they revered the institution and would not let it be tampered with. This attitude persists today, and Presidents ignore it at their peril.

Of our recent Presidents, I believe that Harry Truman had the purest concept of responsibility to the office itself and to the people. He never cared, or acted as though he cared, what history might say about him. This contrasts with statements by Presidents Johnson and Nixon that neither would be the first to lose a war. A President should not be concerned with what history will say of him, but rather with what it will say of his country. President Truman understood this.

Truman openly challenged General Douglas MacArthur, a most popular general, removed him from his command, and following that allowed the General full freedom to express his political views. In his controversy with the steel industry, Truman acted directly to take it over, but then yielded to the Supreme Court when it said he could not do so.

President Truman also had a proper concern for the role of the Vice President. He did not talk of giving the office new meaning. He avoided institutionalizing the office of presidential adviser. No one adviser had a special status or could claim to be the inside man, as was to be the case with Walt Rostow and Henry Kissinger under later Presidents.

The President must have a proper sense of his relationship to the Congress. No President, for example, can function without the support - or at least the cooperation - of the House Ways and Means Committee.

A President generally cannot conduct foreign policy successfully when the Senate Foreign Relations Committee opposes him. President Truman recognized this fact and worked with the Committee, particularly with Senators Arthur Vandenberg and Tom Connally. Senator Vandenberg's support was essential for most of the important postwar programs: the United Nations, the United Nations Relief and Rehabilitation Administration (UNRRA), the Greek-Turkish aid program, and the Marshall Plan. The Vandenberg Resolution, adopted on June 11, 1948, allowed the Truman administration to move ahead with confidence in the negotiations leading to the North Atlantic Treaty. Dean Acheson later wrote that the resolution "made possible the North Atlantic Treaty."[7] Acheson explained:

> *All too often the executive, having sweated through the compromises of a difficult negotiation, had laid the resulting treaty before a quite detached, uninformed, and unresponsive Senate in which a minority could reject the executive's agreement. On this occasion Senator Vandenberg took seriously and responsibly the word "advice" in the constitutional phrase giving the President power to enter into treaties "with the advice*

---

[7] Dean Acheson, <u>Present at the Creation</u> (New York, 1969), p. 266.

29

and consent of the Senate." By getting the Senate to give advice in advance of negotiation he got it to accept responsibility in advance of giving its consent to ratification.... [8]

In recent years there has been no real consultation. The practice has been either to defuse opposition by getting the Senate to sign a blank check in the form of a general resolution or else to proceed without any consultation.

Under the three administrations preceding that of President Nixon, use of the congressional resolution in support of foreign policy was carried to the limit and beyond. Congress passed resolutions under President Eisenhower on Taiwan (1955) and the Middle East (1957); under President Kennedy on Berlin (1962) and Cuba (1962); and under President Johnson on Southeast Asia (1964).

Most of these resolutions related to areas of traditional American interest, such as Taiwan and Berlin, and did not open the door to a significant expansion of the American commitment. The Middle East Resolution of 1957 (the Eisenhower Doctrine) was of a different character: it did allow a significant expansion of the American commitment in an area which was not of traditional American interest. The case of the Tonkin Gulf Resolution in 1964 was also special. It was presented as a response to what was said to be unprovoked attack on innocent American ships in international waters. It later turned out to have been something different from that.

The issue of presidential leadership might be put in better perspective if we speak of a responsible presidency rather than a strong presidency. There are several things that make a responsible presidency.

First is the responsibility to the office itself. The presidency belongs to the country and to the people more than does any other political office. Senators are elected from their respective states and Representatives from their congressional districts. The President is elected by the entire nation.

The President must be sensitive to the needs of the country. But he should understand the limits of politics and government to satisfy many of those needs. He should look on the presidency as an instrument through which ways can be opened to the people and to institutions to

---

[8] ibid.

make their full contribution toward justice and order and happiness.

Even though the President must sometimes give firm leadership, he should understand that this country as a rule does not need so much leadership, because the potential for leadership in a free country must exist in every citizen. Sensing the will of the people, the President must be prepared to move out ahead so that the people can follow, giving direction to the country and guiding it, largely by way of setting people free.

Leadership should be almost a residual function of the office. The more important function is to give direction to the forces running in the country which can be expressed in political action. It is most important to set free the energies - intellectual and spiritual and moral - that exist in America.

It is my belief that for effective government in the twentieth century, the presidency must first of all be depersonalized. We do not need Presidents who are bigger than the country, but rather ones who will speak for it and support it.

The disposition to look upon the presidency as a splendid misery or a monarchy must be revised.

The constitutional relations among the various branches of government must be redefined and then respected. We must return to the founding fathers' concept of the presidency as an office of significant, but limited, power. It must again be an office that shares both power and responsibility with the other branches of government and with the people.

The procedures and practices of our political parties must be reformed in order to make them truly responsible agents of the public.

If these things are done, there will be less need to talk about "strong" or "weak" Presidents. The conditions for effective leadership, including restraint in the use of power, will again be built into the presidency.

The presidency will be returned to the people.

The Vice President as Crown Prince

Throughout most of our history, the Vice President has been either ignored or ridiculed. Many Vice Presidents have themselves joined in the general downgrading. John

31

Adams, who was George Washington's Vice President, said that "my country has, in its wisdom, contrived for me the most insignificant office that ever the invention of man contrived or his imagination conceived; and as I can do neither good nor evil, I must be borne away by others and meet the common fate."[9]

In 1848 some people thought Daniel Webster might accept his party's vice-presidential nomination. But Webster told his daughter that he was allowed to be the first farmer in his area, "and I am content with this, unless I should be called to be first, elsewhere, where I can do more good."[10]

Many years later Mr. Dooley wondered why "ivrybody runs away fr'm a nommynation f'r vice-prisidint as if it was an indictment be th' gran' jury."[11]

Richard Nixon, after serving in the vice-presidency, called that office a "hollow shell - the most ill-conceived, poorly defined position in the American political system."[12]

How the office developed is not entirely clear. The Constitutional Convention left few notes behind to explain it, and Alexander Hamilton noted in The Federalist Papers that the office "has been objected to as superfluous, if not mischievous."[13]

In recent years, "giving new meaning to the vice-presidency" has become a popular slogan. In the Eisenhower administration it was said that Vice President Nixon would be given special assignments and responsibilities. The value of this was brought into question during a 1960 Eisenhower news conference. Someone asked for an example of a major Nixon idea that

[9] John Adams, Letters of John Adams Addressed to His Wife, ed. by Charles Francis Adams (Boston, 1841), Vol. 11, p. 133, letter of December 19, 1793, to Abigail Adams.

[10] Daniel Webster, The Writings and Speeches of Daniel Webster, ed. by Fletcher Webster (Boston, 1903), Vol. XVIII, p. 270, letter of February 14, 1848, to Mrs. J. W. Appleton.

[11] Finley Peter Dunne, Dissertations by Mr. Dooley (New York, 1906), p. 115.

[12] Richard M. Nixon, "The Second Choice," in The 1964 World Book Year Book (Chicago, 1964), p. 80.

[13] Alexander Hamilton, James Madison, and John Jay, The Federalist Papers, No. 68.

the President had adopted. Eisenhower replied, "If you give me a week, I might think of one. I don't remember."[14]

President Kennedy gave special administrative assignments to his Vice President, Lyndon Johnson. Johnson was said to have more responsibilities in government than any other Vice President in history. Yet he was not a happy Vice President.

Vice President Hubert Humphrey publicly acknowledged that he was the agent of the President and that what the President stood for he also stood for.

Vice President Spiro Agnew, through his rhetoric and through his attacks on the media, students, intellectuals, and politicians, gave another new meaning to the office during President Nixon's first term. He was, it was observed, "Nixon's Nixon."

Vice President Gerald Ford held the office too briefly for new meanings.

If we take it for granted that the vice-presidency should be given new meaning, we must assume it has an old meaning that should be changed, or that the office never had any real meaning and had better get one soon.

Despite all these comments, the office is a most important one. This is true even though the Vice President's only official duties are to preside over the Senate (a duty for the most part taken by Senate members themselves) and to cast the deciding vote in the rare event of a tie.

The real importance of the office rests on the fact that the Vice President assumes the presidency in the case of the death or disability of the President. Of the forty-five Vice Presidents, eight succeeded to office because the President died in office. One succeeded because the President resigned. Five others were later elected to the presidency. Thus, altogether, about one third of those who have held the office have subsequently become President. Vice Presidents, therefore, should be chosen with care.

Political parties and presidential candidates often have shown little concern for the ability of their vice-presidential candidates. In some conventions, the candidate offers the vice-presidency to the governor of a politically important state or to a politician who has the support of a number of states. Or he may offer it to

---

[14] Public Papers of the Presidents: Dwight D. Eisenhower, 1960-61 (Washington, 1961), p. 658, news conference of August 24, 1960.

someone of religious or ethnic background different from his own in order to "balance" the ticket.

Results of last-minute and rather careless selections have caused many problems in campaigns and in the office itself, and the vice-presidency generally seems to have a bad effect on the individuals who serve in it. Perhaps we should abolish the office and provide another method of succession, such as selection of a new President by the Congress or by the people.

If the vice-presidency is retained in our system, however, selections for the office must be improved. Ideally, the person chosen to be Vice President should be as well qualified for the presidency as the person he may succeed. In fact, the presidential candidate should be modest enough to look for someone better qualified than himself. The Vice President should be selected with more attention to his native ability and less attention to his native state, his religion, or the impact of his television personality.

If the Vice President is used properly, and if he uses his own time well, he should become more aware of the problems facing the nation and be better prepared to deal with them than a President without previous experience in the executive branch. By conducting himself with dignity and reserve in the vice-presidency, he might be accepted by the nation, if he becomes President, with fewer partisan identifications and political scars than the person he succeeds.

A Vice President should not be used principally as a defender of presidential policies. Under ordinary circumstances he should not be used as an administrative officer. He should not be distracted by unnecessary assignments or by irrelevant jobs that could be done by other officials. He should not be sent on hopeless missions. He should not be required to do the President's dirty jobs or to stir up partisan fervor and division in the country.

A Vice President should be treated much as a crown prince is treated in a monarchy. He should be trained in the arts of government. He should not be used in the temporary and transient affairs of the government. He should be protected from partisan strife.

The holder of that office should use it to make the office more honorable and to make himself respected by the people.

Of recent Vice Presidents, Alben Barkley best met these standards. He was not Truman's assistant President. His relations with the Senate were excellent. His influence was strong, although he made no claim to power or special privilege. His public image was one of repose and restraint. His partisanship was always pleasant and minimal. There was no talk during his term of giving "new meaning" to the office. It was accepted that, had the emergency arisen, he could have become an entirely satisfactory President.

To stand by as a potential President of the United States is a sufficient burden in itself. This view of the office was stated most properly by Thomas Jefferson, when he was Vice President: "The second office of the government is honorable and easy. . . ."[15] It would give him, he said, "philosophical evenings in the winter, and rural days in summer."[16]

Changes in the Congress

The complaint that Congress is recalcitrant or derelict or ineffective in responding to administration proposals is often heard in the land. Criticism of Congress is usually popular and reflects traditional American attitudes and theories of government. It is also a reaction to current failings of governmental institutions and officials.

President Truman by his criticism made famous the "Republican 'do-nothing' 80th Congress."[17] President Nixon was less harsh when he accused the Ninety-first Congress of "turn-of-the-century"[18] work schedules and procedures. But stronger was the criticism he aimed at the Senate. "In the final months and weeks of 1970,"[19] he said, "... the nation was presented with the spectacle of a

---

[15] Thomas Jefferson, The Writings of Thomas Jefferson, ed. by Andrew A. Lipscomb (Washington, 1903), Vol. IX, p. 381, letter of May 13, 1797, to Elbridge Gerry.

[16] ibid., p. 374, letter of January 22, 1797, to Dr. Benjamin Rush.

[17] Public Papers of the Presidents: Harry S. Truman, 1948 (Washington, 1964), pp. 518 and 573, campaign speeches of September 1948.

[18] Public Papers of the Presidents: Richard Nixon, 1971 (Washington, 1972), p. 25, statement of January 5, 1971.

[19] ibid., p. 24.

legislative body that had seemingly lost the capacity to decide and the will to act. When the path was finally cleared, vital days had been lost, and major failures insured."

President Nixon's criticism of the Ninety-second Congress related principally to the issue of federal spending. He charged that Congress had been on a spending spree. In his 1972 campaign, Mr. Nixon promised to avoid a "Presidential tax increase," but warned that free spending by Congress could produce a "Congressional tax increase."[20] This obscured the fact that Nixon's chief difference with the Ninety-second Congress was over priorities. The President had insisted on high military spending, while the Congress had demanded more money for domestic needs. It was the combination of the two demands that had produced large deficits.

In the 1974 congressional campaign President Ford complained of congressional spending, but wound up asking that the country give him only enough supporters in the Congress so that his vetoes might be sustained. It was the least request any President had made of the voters.

The temptation to denounce Congress in all its works and all its pomps is understandable. A great part of every session's work is routine, and much is trivial. I recall a day when the Senate had a roll-call vote on changing a typographical error. There was another occasion when it held a great debate on the gold standard. Everyone was there except William Jennings Bryan. He should have been there - we needed him. The gold debate had not advanced very far since his day.

The few minutes of evening television devoted to the work of Congress are reserved for the more sensational committee hearings or short accounts of final action on major legislative proposals. The image is often one of uncertainty, confusion, and contradiction.

Members of Congress are responsible in some degree for the tendency to judge the work of Congress by quantity rather than quality. To justify their stewardship, some of them fill many pages of the Congressional Record with irrelevant statistics about laws enacted, nominations confirmed, roll-call votes, and the days and

---

[20] Public Papers of the President: Richard Nixon, 1972 (Washington, 1974), p. 958, news conference of October 5, 1972.

hours spent in session. Since Congress has been in almost continuous session for the past decade, the numbers alone are impressive but not necessarily enlightening.

Neither presidential rhetoric nor reports about quantity of legislation provide the standard by which to judge the effectiveness of Congress. Overstatement of existing weaknesses and extravagant claims of what may be accomplished through procedural reform will contribute little to a proper understanding of the role of Congress. A closer look at the role of the Senate in recent years will contribute much more.

In 1957 William S. White published a book on the United States Senate. The Senate of The Citadel was a place, according to Mr. White, "upon whose vitality and honor will at length rest the whole issue of the kind of society that we are to maintain."[21] Mr. White, after examining the Senate of those days, found it to be good. He evaluated the members of the Senate and found many of them to be giants among men. He examined the rules of procedure and found them wholly satisfactory and appropriate, if not inspired, and sanctioned beyond time and history.

The popular judgment of the United States Senate today is something quite different from that of William S. White in the mid-1950s. The Senate is charged with failing to meet its responsibilities, being unresponsive to national needs, confused and incompetent, tangled in its own rules, and serving at best as a platform from which to launch presidential campaigns.

At times the Senate seems to be the last primitive society. It has great respect for seniority, which is of primitive disposition. It has great respect for occupancy and for the territorial imperative; you can scarcely move a senator out of an office, even after he has died. And the Senate has its own trial by ordeal, which is called the filibuster.

The Senate of today is not the Senate of 1957; neither is it the Senate as described in popular criticism. Despite certain similarities to a primitive society, it is more than that. Working under difficult circumstances, it has in recent times made a record of positive achievement.

When I entered the Senate in 1959, the reputedly strong men of the past - Democrats like Tom Connally of

---

[21] William S. White, The Citadel (New York, 1957), p. x.

Texas and Walter George of Georgia - were gone. And on the Republican side, such stalwarts as the senior Robert Taft of Ohio, Arthur Vandenberg of Michigan, Eugene Millikin of Colorado, and others listed by White were gone. The Senate had new leaders, new members, and new problems.

In the years immediately following World War II, the Senate was involved in settling the postwar world. It ratified the peace treaties and helped establish the United Nations, the North Atlantic Treaty Organization, and the Marshall Plan. These were important tasks that the Senate performed well.

In this same period, especially after 1948, the Senate was largely immobilized in dealing with domestic problems because nearly every issue - whether it was housing, education, or whatever - became a civil-rights issue. And on civil rights the Senate was deadlocked. Consequently, from 1948 until 1959, the House of Representatives generally pushed ahead of the Senate in dealing with domestic problems.

A significant change occurred in the elections of 1958. In that year twelve new senators, liberal on most domestic issues, were elected: E. L. Bartlett of Alaska, Thomas Dodd of Connecticut, Clair Engle of California, Ernest Gruening of Alaska, Philip Hart of Michigan, Vance Hartke of Indiana, Gale McGee of Wyoming, Frank Moss of Utah, Edmund Muskie of Maine, Harrison Williams of New Jersey, Stephen Young of Ohio, and myself. The immediate effect was that the initiative on most domestic issues shifted from the House to the Senate. Now the Senate began to move ahead of the House in advocating new legislative programs, increasing appropriations to support established programs, and facing the civil-rights issue. But it was not until the 1964 presidential election, when the Goldwater candidacy gave the House a clear liberal majority, that the Congress as a whole could deal with the great mass of domestic legislation that had needed action for many years.

The Senate's concern with domestic problems had both good and bad effects. The good effect was that much necessary legislation was passed. The bad effects were two.

First, preoccupation with domestic problems made the Senate fail to give proper attention to international relations. As a result, there was the gradual usurpation of power in this field by the - executive branch of the government through the use of executive agreements and executive actions without formal treaties. In some cases, these merely continued wartime relationships. But new commitments - legal or extralegal - were made during the time that John Foster Dulles was Secretary of State and his brother Allen was head of the Central Intelligence Agency.

The second bad effect of the Senate's concern with domestic problems was the change in the structure and operation of the Senate. This occurred especially while Lyndon Johnson was Majority Leader. The Senate became a kind of upper House of Representatives, with emphasis on committee work, roll calls, and quantitative measurements of success. Senator Johnson often announced the number of bills passed and made comparisons with other Congresses, both in terms of timing and in terms of the volume of legislative action. (Johnson's attitude toward both houses of Congress caused him problems in the later years of his presidency. He had experience in driving cattle, where the technique is to start the cattle slowly and then stampede them at the end. But when you deal with Congress, you should know about the psychology of pigs, which is opposite that of cattle. In driving hogs, you start them as fast as you can, you make all kinds of noise, and you try to panic them. You shout at them in Latin. But once they are started, you slow them as you go along. When you get them right up to the pen you want them in, you come to a stop. The pigs will then look right and left and think that they have discovered it. And in they go.) There also are some issues requiring human respect.

The Senate's influence on foreign policy was further weakened by the development of the cold war into an ideological conflict and the formalization of that conflict in comprehensive treaties like the Southeast Asia Treaty Organization (SEATO) and in resolutions like that on the Gulf of Tonkin in 1964. Congressional criticism was thus stifled, and congressional power yielded to the executive sometimes even in advance of any defined problem, as in the case of the Middle East Resolution, passed under President Eisenhower in 1957.

The Senate itself in these years was a victim of the cold war. The immediate manifestation of this was its intimidation by Senator Joseph McCarthy and his two or three active supporters in the Senate. Both the Senate and the State Department retreated in the face of their challenge.

At the same time, the influence of the military over foreign policy increased greatly. American military missions were set up in many countries and were used more and more as instruments of foreign policy. The military establishment also gained strength in other ways. As its strength grew, diplomatic and even strategic considerations received less and less attention. The disposition to consider military action as the solution to nearly every problem became dominant.

A third force which in this period also weakened the Senate's role in foreign policy - a force which the Senate should have recognized and challenged early - was the inclusion or intrusion of the House into the field of foreign policy making. This occurred in two ways. It happened directly because the Marshall Plan and other aid programs required authorization and appropriation of money by the House as well as the Senate. And it arose indirectly from the continued support by the House of a military establishment larger and stronger than was favored by the Senate. Both President Johnson and President Nixon encouraged the shift of power to the House. Johnson turned to the House for support in Vietnam. Nixon encouraged the adoption there of the Hays resolution in 1969, which affirmed House support of the President in his efforts to achieve "a just peace in Vietnam"[22] and passed by a vote of 333 to 55. Thereafter President Nixon often depended on the House to blunt the effect of Senate opposition to the war.

Only with the escalation of the war in Southeast Asia did the Senate begin to give serious attention to what had happened to it and to reassert its rights and responsibilities in the field of foreign policy. The road back has been difficult. Much of the high ground had been lost to the executive branch and the military, and low ground to the House of Representatives.

But the Senate has begun to fight back. The effort has been not so much one of individual leaders or even of the "club" (the inner circle that supposedly controls the Senate). Essentially, it has been a response of the whole Senate.

---

[22] *Congressional Record*, December 2, 1969, p. 36536.

In the 1960s the Foreign Relations Committee challenged the independence of the Central Intelligence Agency. The committee won a small concession within the Senate when it was agreed that a few members of Foreign Relations would join members of Armed Services and Appropriations on what was called an intelligence "oversight committee." There was more truth than was intended in that committee title. Senator Fulbright noted that the CIA would only tell you what it wanted to tell you anyway. (And some senators did not want to know everything. One of them said, "Just don't tell me; I don't want to know of it." Others on the supervisory committee say, "If you knew what we know ..." Senators who say that should be taken off the committee; they have been at the front too long.)

Another development in the late 1960s and early 1970s was a stronger assertion of responsibility by the Senate. For the first time since the expansion of the military after World War II, the Congress, but especially the Senate and more particularly Senator William Proxmire - raised serious and effective challenges to military spending. Despite strong resistance by the executive, they were able to make some cuts in the military budget and to slow development of the antiballistic missile system. Opposition to the ABM system reflected not just military, scientific, and economic considerations but also a significant change in foreign policy views.

The device of the congressional resolution as a means of supporting administration policy was repudiated. In 1966 only five senators voted to take up the Tonkin Gulf Resolution for reconsideration and possible repeal. In 1970 only five senators voted against repeal on the final vote. One can rightly say that repeal came after the resolution had been fully used; nevertheless, it had symbolic importance as an indication of Senate awareness.

There were many other Senate efforts to limit or end the war. These actions were largely negative and after the fact. Even the antiwar amendments that passed the Senate were generally rejected by the House. Yet the Senate helped pressure the Nixon administration to withdraw United States troops from Vietnam. Both houses finally forced an end to the bombing of Cambodia in 1973.

In the Senate's effort to reclaim its constitutional role in foreign policy, much credit must go to recent members of the Foreign Relations Committee: Democrats like J. William Fulbright and Frank Church, and Republicans like Clifford Case and John Sherman Cooper. Special credit must go to some of the relatively new Republican members of the Senate - such men as Mark Hatfield of Oregon, Richard Schweiker of Pennsylvania, Charles Mathias of Maryland - who have shown greater concern for the constitutional role of the Senate in this field than they have for uncritical party loyalty.

Another area of responsibility in which the Senate has made an important record in recent years is improving the federal judiciary. Although the initiative came principally from the executive, the Senate sustained and encouraged presidential efforts to improve the courts. During the terms of Presidents Truman, Eisenhower, Kennedy, and Johnson, the nation gradually began to move away from what until that time was a regional judicial system. There was one system for the North, another for the South, one for the Northeast, another for the Southwest. The practice was to clear all judges for a district court with the senators in that jurisdiction. It was almost as though senators were permitted to say to other senators, "You can have whatever kind of justice you want in your state if you leave us alone in ours."

Civil rights was the principal cause for the change of emphasis. But the Senate also recognized that the country had been unified by many economic and social factors as well as by greater mobility of the people.

President Johnson's 1965 nomination of a former Mississippi governor for appointment to the Fifth Circuit was thoroughly challenged on the civil-rights issue. Other nominees to the circuit courts were checked carefully. Also in 1965, a Johnson nominee for the District Court of Massachusetts was so strongly opposed on the ground of competence that the nominee's name was withdrawn.

President Johnson's 1968 nomination of Abe Fortas as Chief Justice of the United States was challenged by senators who alleged conflict of interest. There was a filibuster against the nomination, and Johnson eventually withdrew it.

The Senate in 1969 and 1970 rejected two of President Nixon's nominees for the Supreme Court. In turning down the Haynsworth and Carswell nominations, the Senate clearly showed that it was not prepared to accept the Nixon theory of a Supreme Court on which regional differences were to be represented. The Senate preferred a national court whose members would be selected as qualified to deal with national problems on a national scale. Senator Birch Bayh of Indiana led the fight against the appointment of Judge Haynsworth and then, almost alone in the early days, against the appointment of Judge Carswell.

At the same time the Judiciary Committee, and especially Senator Sam Ervin of North Carolina, patiently and persistently defended the right of privacy and the right of every citizen to due process.

Much remains to be done. The House of Representatives has made steps toward greater efficiency and responsibility. The Senate is slow, sometimes tedious, irritating to the press, to the country, to its own members. Yet as that instrument of government in which the men who wrote the Constitution placed residual or shared responsibility for all governmental actions executive, legislative, and judicial - the Senate has done reasonably well. The Senate and House have set up a Congressional Budget Office a hopeful sign.

The most serious immediate test of democracy and American political process is outside the Senate and outside the House. It rests in more responsible political parties and more responsible and relevant presidential elections.

The Courts, the Last-Appeal

It seems that almost every problem we have today eventually goes to court for solution. Many go to the Supreme Court for the final word. Whether it is an issue of delegate selection within a political party or an order telling a protest group to move off the Mall in Washington, it goes to the Supreme Court. When the justices meet on the issue of driving Vietnam veterans off the Mall, we have an activist court, despite what Warren Burger might wish.

In our society the last test and last line of defense is in the courts. It is at this level that the right of due process must be safeguarded at all costs. But the courts today are severely overburdened, a condition that weakens them as the last line of defense. The principal causes of this condition are more complex than the often cited ones of "too many appeals" or "too few judges."

Changing the physical shape of the bench in the Supreme Court from a straight to a shallow inverted U form is not likely to help much - though it may, as Chief Justice Burger said, enable the justices to see which one of them is talking. (We have long believed that justice is blind, not deaf.)

The obvious question is: Why do so many issues go to court?

I think one reason is that most of our institutions are not operating properly. An institution is really a formalization of law in which people find that, by applying reasonable rules of conduct and accepting that they must make some concessions, a tolerable accommodation is possible. Today this is not the case in many areas of American life. Institutions that formerly resolved disputes in the manner of a community now find themselves in court. Stockholders are suing directors of their own corporations. Patients are suing doctors for malpractice. Universities are sued by students and by athletes. Churches are sued by dissident members on the issue of who owns the church. The Little League was taken to court to force it to let girls play in its games.

A second reason is that the complexity of life today calls for redefining basic liberties guaranteed by the Bill of Rights. Freedom of speech and press is now something quite different from what it was in the early days of the Republic. Then it meant the right to say something in a public square or to publish a newspaper or pamphlet. Now it must also deal with government withholding of information and with concentrated control of newspapers and broadcast media.

Freedom of assembly then related to rather simple meetings of people; now it must cover things such as demonstrations, protest marches, and the right to belong to protest groups. It must also be applied to the current government definition of conspiracy. There is a new Scripture on this: if two or more people are gathered in anyone's name, it is a conspiracy. It is not a religious rally but something quite different. And if two people agree upon things together, they may be subject to prosecution. If you think of it all alone, you are relatively safe. If you happen to think of it at the same time that someone else does, you may be in danger.

When the Bill of Rights was adopted, the right of privacy was a matter of insisting on search warrants and not allowing the government to quarter troops in your home. Today it is challenged by complicated technological devices for spying on people. We have found something new about telephones, for example. You do not even have to pick up the receiver; they report all the time to central headquarters.

A third reason for the burden on the courts is the failure of other institutions to meet their most basic responsibilities. This is a failure quite apart from the general institutional breakdown.

The failure of Congress and the President to take the initiative on civil rights forced the courts to act. This often meant that there was no administrative machinery or supporting legislation to sustain the court decisions. So there was an imbalance between what the courts ordered and what was carried out. The result was great friction, as in the case of busing. A similar problem developed with due process guarantees.

Political parties have also been at fault. A simple proposition like "one person, one vote" should have been reflected in the party process long ago. Yet as late as 1972, the courts were faced with lawsuits over allocation of delegates by state, over the winner-take-all primary in California, and over a credentials challenge in Illinois. Had the parties met their responsibility, the courts would not have become involved in these disputes.

A fourth reason the courts are overburdened is that Congress has failed to bring old laws up to date. And it has passed some bad laws and also some that are uncertain and almost inapplicable. The drug laws are outdated; the penalties for marijuana use, for example, are absurd. Much of our antitrust legislation has no significant reference to current problems.

A fifth reason for the burden on the courts is the failure of the executive branch to enforce laws as passed and as interpreted by the courts. Nixon's and Ford's statements and actions on busing, for example, encouraged resistance to court orders. Some executive agencies have refused to comply with the Freedom of Information Act until forced to do so by the courts. The Justice Department at times has defied the law dealing with wiretaps.

Besides creating unnecessary cases for the courts, such actions have undermined the law itself. As Felix Frankfurter once wrote, "The contrast between morality professed by society and immorality practiced on its behalf makes for contempt of law. Respect for law cannot be turned off and on as though it were a hotwater faucet."[23]

Recent administrations have also thrown a great burden on the court system by prosecution of political dissenters for "conspiracy." The Johnson administration moved against Dr. Benjamin Spock and others for an alleged conspiracy to promote draft resistance. The Nixon administration pressed a number of conspiracy cases. Some of them, like the prosecution of the Berrigans and others for an alleged attempt to kidnap Henry Kissinger, made the government and the country look ridiculous.

The prosecution of Daniel Ellsberg for his release of the Pentagon Papers was also unnecessary. The government could have resolved that case by arresting the Xerox machine, placing it in jail, and eventually having a ceremonial execution.

Finally, there are failures in the court system itself - some inherent in it and some a consequence of personalities and other forces.

The Nixon administration aggravated problems in the system by proposing regional representation and "balance" on the Supreme Court. There was much resistance to this concept of the Court, and with good reason. If the Nixon approach were applied to the federal judiciary, it would impose upon it the very concept rejected in a twenty-year effort to establish a national system of justice.

Chief Justice Warren Burger appears to have a concept of administered justice which could also add to the existing difficulties of the courts. He has manifested great concern about expediting cases and reforming the lower courts. Mr. Burger's view of the court system is close to the tradition and practice in England, which has a court system directed from the top down. This is not our tradition.

The principal concern of the Chief Justice and his associates should be the difficult area of constitutional

---

[23] Felix Frankfurter, dissenting opinion in *Lee v. United States*, in *United States Reports* (Washington, 1952), Vol. CCCXLIII, pp. 758 59.

law. While they attend to that, the Congress and the President and the people should reduce the general burden on the courts by reforming the laws and practices of the country and rebuilding institutional relations.

Court of Ideas

Alexis de Tocqueville, in commenting on American political and governmental institutions in the 1830s, observed with regard to the United States Supreme Court that "a mightier judicial authority has never been constituted in any land."[24] And then, after listing some powers of the Court, he made this profound point concerning it: "One might even say that its prerogatives are entirely political, although its constitution is purely judicial."[25]

Gradually, and without much reflection, we have come to accept the idea that all judges should be selected from the legal profession. A case can be made for appointing lawyers to preside over lower courts, where most cases are settled within the limits of the law as written or as interpreted by the courts. It might even be argued that creative imagination or a disposition to make legal judgments within the broader context of history and philosophy is not desirable in the lower courts.

A similar case cannot be made for the appointment of lawyers to the Supreme Court.

Cases involving simple points of law are ordinarily not taken to the Supreme Court. If a case involving a point of law is accepted, it usually requires a decision that is beyond the law as defined. Most of the Supreme Court's important decisions do not deal with technical legal distinctions or definitions. In performing their most important function, Supreme Court judges do not "think or speak as lawyers." The judgments they are called upon to make are much broader and deeper; they are beyond the "limits" of the law.

Students of constitutional history and of the Supreme Court usually identify three periods in American constitutional development: the first, from 1789 to the end

---

[24] Alexis de Tocqueville, Democracy in America, ed. by J. P. Mayer (Garden City, N.Y., 1969), p. 149.

[25] ibid., p. 150.

of the Civil War, in which the Court's role in interpreting the Constitution and its application in changing circumstances was established; the second, from 1865 to the "Court revolution" of 1937, during which the Court was preoccupied with property rights and "the law"; and the third (allowing for the interruption of World War II), taking up where the Court had left off in the late 1930s.

The record of the Court in the first and second periods confirms Mr. Dooley's observation that the Supreme Court "follows th' iliction returns," and also the more respectful judgment of historians that the Court in those years responded to necessity and to a reading of what the country would accept.

The same cannot be said of the Court today. In part because of political failure in the presidency and in the Congress, and in part because the movement of history and the demand for change have accelerated, the Court has moved to take the initiative - or has been forced to take it - in critical areas of law and constitutional interpretation.

The test today is more difficult than the tests of the past. The earlier tests did not pit the Constitution against common practice; they involved confrontation at the pragmatic level rather than the level of theory or philosophy. Today the confrontation is between two concepts of law. One flows from the common law; it involves precedent and traditional relationships, such as those between husband and wife, parent and child, master and servant, rights in property. The other flows from the rationalistic and individualistic concept written into the Constitution. This sustains the proposition of the Declaration of Independence that all men are created equal, have the same rights under the law, and are to be given the same protection.

Narrow training in law - case studies and reliance on precedents - is of little help in dealing with a legal challenge of a different kind. In fact, such training may be a handicap. There is need for more than a knowledge of legal precedents and procedures. The areas into which the court has moved - and ones into which it must move - require as a base for sound judgment a knowledge of history, philosophy, and other disciplines.

The judges and lawyers in the early years of the United States were not educated in a system of narrow professional definition or professional curriculum. In colonial and postcolonial times, the study of law was incidental to broader liberal education. When John Adams was admitted to the bar in Massachusetts in 1758, he was introduced this way: "Of Mr. Adams, as he is unknown to your Honours, It is necessary to say that he has lived between 2 and 3 Years with Mr. Putnam of Worcester, has a good Character from him, and all others who know him, and that he was with me the other day several Hours, and I take it he is qualified to study the Law by his scholarship..."[26] (Adams had graduated A.B. 1755 from Harvard.)

That a judge is "thinking as a lawyer" or "speaking as a lawyer" is not a reassuring statement when the subject matter is human rights in an age of nuclear biology. It is easier for a historian or a philosopher to seek legal counsel when needed than it is for a lawyer to seek historical and philosophical counsel and evaluate that counsel when he needs it.

The Constitution sets no barriers to the appointment of nonlawyers to the Supreme Court. The times argue for the appointment of nonlawyers or of lawyers who have established themselves in some broader field - persons like Henry Steele Commager, Barbara Tuchman, David Riesman, and Hannah Arendt.

A Kind Word for the Bureaucrats

Whereas the public and telling show down on Watergate and related activities came in the courts, with some support from the Watergate Committee of the Senate and the Judiciary Committee of the House, the first challenges came within the federal agencies and bureaus.

It is not clear from the record whether personal integrity, respect for the law, loyalty to the agency, protection of self within the context of the agency, or some combination of the above was the compelling motivation for resistance. Nonetheless, it is reassuring to know that there was a line at which presidential power was challenged, its thrust blunted and even turned back by civil servants and political appointees.

---

[26] John Adams Diary and Autobiography of John Adams, ed. by L. H. Butterfield (Cambridge, Mass., 1961), Vol. I, p. 58.

One might have expected the Federal Bureau of Investigation to have resisted presidential intervention more quickly and more strongly than other agencies. It has a tradition of independence. It is a part of the Justice Department, where integrity against political pressure has some standing.

If J. Edgar Hoover had been alive and in charge of the FBI during the Watergate months, the response of the Bureau would certainly have been different, although not necessarily better. A recent report shows that from the early 1960s until April 1971 the FBI conducted programs of disruption and harassment against such groups as the Socialist Workers Party, black nationalist organizations, and the Southern Christian Leadership Conference. Perhaps J. Edgar Hoover could have been convinced that the Democratic party in 1972 was radical enough to deserve the attention of his Bureau.

In any case, the FBI under the direction of L. Patrick Gray came off rather badly in the face of the first White House pressure. Gray lacked experience, security, or backbone to resist White House pressures. How else could one explain his taking personal custody of the files of E. Howard Hunt, one of the Watergate burglars, and burning them? His early concern seemed to be more over jurisdictional lines between the FBI and the CIA than over the right or wrong of his operations. The record indicates that Gray finally found his level, and held a line, at the time of his resignation. Resistance at lower levels of the FBI apparently consisted largely of leaking to the press information which indicated that a cover-up was in progress.

As for the rest of the Justice Department, the record in the early stages of Watergate was not good. Assistant Attorney General Henry Petersen and the original Watergate prosecutors did a less than adequate job in their investigation. The prosecutors, of course, were in a difficult spot, carrying the case against - or anticipating, at least, that they would have to carry their case against - high officials of their own government. They contend that their strategy of first convicting the burglars, then immunizing them and forcing them to testify, was working at the time that the Senate Watergate Committee and the Special Prosecutor took over the investigation. It may have been; but the prosecutors neglected other possibilities for breaking the case in the first six months of their investigation. Petersen's justification for his reporting grandjury actions to the President is acceptable only if one believes that the President has rights that do not apply to other persons involved, likely to be involved, or having an interest in criminal prosecutions.

The record of Attorney General Richard Kleindienst - if one excepts his 1972 failure to tell the Senate Judiciary Committee the truth about White House intervention in the International Telephone and Telegraph (ITT) antitrust case, which resulted in his subsequent guilty plea to a misdemeanor and in a light probationary sentence was good. As Attorney General, he withstood White House pressures a number of times. When G. Gordon Liddy, one of the "plumbers," found Kleindienst at the Burning Tree Country Club shortly after the Watergate break-in and told him that some of the burglars might be employed by the White House or the Committee for the Re-election of the President, Kleindienst responded immediately by calling Henry Petersen and telling him that the Watergate burglars were to be treated exactly as anyone else would be under similar circumstances. Kleindienst then, according to report, told Liddy to leave the club or go to hell, or words to that effect.

Either on Petersen's advice or in agreement with him, Kleindienst refused to supply John Dean with FBI reports on the Watergate investigation. The reports were given to Dean by L. Patrick Gray without Kleindienst's knowledge.

When, in July or August 1972, John Ehrlichman, chief domestic affairs adviser to President Nixon, called Kleindienst to complain that Henry Petersen had refused to carry out an order from Ehrlichman, Kleindienst responded - as an Attorney General should have by asking Ehrlichman why he was talking to Petersen and giving him instructions. He then backed Petersen and directed Ehrlichman never again to attempt to give orders to anyone in the Justice Department. When Ehrlichman refused to concede, according to Kleindienst's testimony, the Attorney General said, "All right, John, if you will not agree to that I will come down Monday, I would like to meet with you and the President, and if the President tells me that you have the authority and the power to give specific instructions to people in the Department of

Justice then I will submit my resignation."[27] At that point, according to Kleindienst, Ehrlichman treated the matter lightly, saying, "Do not get excited, I was only kidding; do not worry about it, it will never happen again."[28] Later Kleindienst testified, "I can say to you that it never did happen again."[29]

In April 1973 President Nixon told Henry Petersen to stay out of the Fielding break-in case because it was a national-security matter. (In 1971 the files of Dr. Lewis Fielding, Daniel Ellsberg's psychiatrist, had been broken into.) Petersen went to the Attorney General with the legal case for disclosing the break-in. Kleindienst studied the issue, agreed with Petersen, and got Nixon to change his position. Petersen later said that he and Kleindienst had agreed beforehand that they would resign if Nixon did not reverse his earlier decision. Kleindienst finally resigned because of potential conflict of interest in directing the prosecution, or being indirectly responsible for the prosecution, of former associates in the administration. Not a bad record under difficult circumstances.

The Internal Revenue Service, like the FBI, showed early weakness, some of it undoubtedly carried over from practices under other administrations. John Caulfield of the White House staff obtained confidential tax information on individuals from former IRS Assistant Commissioner Vernon Acree. This included information on one person under consideration for appointment to the Nixon re-election campaign, on Billy Graham, and on a Newsday reporter who had written an article about Nixon's friend Bebe Rebozo. According to The Washington Post of August 1, 1974, Caulfield's requests were informally made to and answered by Acree. Acree also said, "Other representatives of other administrations sat in my office and read tax returns. It was routine."[30]

The IRS practice of making "sensitive case reports" was mentioned in passing in Watergate-related testimony. "Sensitive case reports" are monthly reports sent to the IRS Commissioner from the field to keep the

[27] U.S. Senate, *Hearings Before the Select Committee on Presidential Campaign Activities . . . Phase I: Watergate Investigation*, Book 9, p. 3565.

[28] ibid.

[29] ibid.

[30] Vernon Acree, quoted in *The Washington Post*, August 1, 1974.

Commissioner and the Secretary of the Treasury informed of IRS investigations or proceedings related to prominent persons or sensitive matters. There is no indication in hearings relative to Watergate that these reports were exploited by the IRS, although the possibility of abuse is present. IRS Commissioner Donald C. Alexander announced in July 1974 that the list of sensitive cases was being changed to include only cases significant for tax administration, instead of including cases characterized by prominence of the taxpayer. He also said that the list no longer circulated outside the IRS.

Even before Watergate, the IRS was showing strength and integrity in the face of Nixon-administration demands. Randolph Thrower, IRS Commissioner in the early years of the Nixon administration stood up to the White House staff on at least two occasions. One involved a leak to the Jack Anderson column of an investigation of Governor George Wallace's brother. Thrower had reason to believe that it had been leaked by or through White House chief of staff, H. R. Haldeman. Thrower and the Chief Counsel of the IRS visited Haldeman and Ehrlichman, discussed the gravity of the matter, and noted that unauthorized disclosure of such information was a criminal offense. They did not make accusations against individuals; perhaps they should have. Haldeman and Ehrlichman, according to Thrower, apparently took the complaint seriously and assured Thrower and his Counsel that they would try to prevent such incidents in the future.

Also in 1970, Thrower was pressured by the White House to appoint John Caulfield to a major IRS job. Thrower concluded that Caulfield was not qualified for it and suggested an alternative position. Initially the White House was not interested in the second job for Caulfield, but it later suggested that he be given the position (Chief of the Enforcement Branch of the Alcohol, Tobacco and Firearms Division) - but that the position be taken out of the normal chain of command so that Caulfield would report directly to Thrower. Thrower opposed this proposition for several reasons. He wanted to keep the Enforcement Branch apolitical. Moreover, Thrower explained, "I was in fact very much concerned about the potential for a personal police force which would not have the protection and insulation of the career staff. Finally, Dr. Walker [Under Secretary of the Treasury] advised that he had been asked by the White House to tell me that all of my views had been taken into account but that I was to be directed to proceed as ... requested. I advised Dr. Walker that he could tell the people at the White House that if they did insist upon the measure I would consider that my usefulness as Commissioner had been terminated. A day or two later Dr. Walker called back to advise that the White House had stated that they would drop the matter."[31][32]

About two months after Thrower had won that battle, he "advised Secretary of the Treasury Kennedy that I would submit my resignation to the President. I told him that I first would like to discuss with the President my concern about White House attitudes toward the IRS, a problem which he [Kennedy] recognized. He told me that as a presidential appointee I had that privilege and said he would arrange the conference. He later advised that he had been unable to arrange the conference and said that Mr. Haldeman had told him that the President did not like such conferences."

Finally Thrower took his complaint to Attorney General John Mitchell, who assured him that the message would be passed on to the President. Thrower then submitted his resignation.

The new Commissioner, Johnnie Walters, was soon subjected to White House pressure for political use of the IRS. He did initiate a check of Democratic National Chairman Lawrence O'Brien's tax returns after receiving the word from the White House (through Secretary of the Treasury George Shultz) that the Democratic leader might not have reported properly, if at all, large amounts of income. Walters found O'Brien's report to be correct, but John Ehrlichman, who had made the original suggestion, was not satisfied with that report. He prompted the IRS to interview O'Brien in connection with an IRS investigation of Howard Hughes. The interview might have been held eventually because of O'Brien's connection with the Hughes organization, but probably would not have been held until after the 1972 election. Instead, it was held in the summer of 1972. Ehrlichman was not satisfied with

---

[31] U.S. House of Representatives, Committee on the Judiciary, *Statement of Information, Book VIII, Internal Revenue Service* (Washington, May June 1974), p. 57, affidavit of Randolph Thrower, May 24, 1974.

[32] ibid., pp. 57 58.

the report of the interview; Shultz so informed Commissioner Walters. Walters told Shultz that the matter was closed. When Shultz and Walters telephoned Ehrlichman to tell him that, Ehrlichman, according to Walters, "indicated disappointment, and said to me 'I'm goddamn tired of your foot-dragging tactics.' "[33]

"I was offended . . ." said Walters. "Following the telephone conversation, I told Secretary Shultz that he could have my job any time he wanted it."[34]

Ehrlichman, in explaining his persistence, said that he believed that the IRS was auditing Republicans at the time but was stalling on an audit of O'Brien when, as he said, "I wanted them to turn up something and send him to jail before the election and unfortunately it didn't materialize."[35]

In September 1972 John Dean gave Commissioner Walters a list of McGovern staff members and contributors and asked that the IRS examine the people on the list. Walters told Dean that such action would be disastrous both for the IRS and for the Nixon administration and that it would make Watergate look like a "Sunday school picnic."[36] Walters said, however, that he would discuss the request with Secretary Shultz and recommend that the IRS do nothing about it. Walters did report to Shultz and showed him the list. Shultz agreed that the IRS should do nothing with it. Nevertheless, Dean followed up with another request, which the IRS ignored.

The IRS did, however, respond to White House pressure to investigate certain organizations. In 1969 presidential aide Tom Charles Huston suggested that the IRS stress checks of leftist groups that might be abusing their tax-exempt status. In response the IRS set up a special task force to check on both leftist and rightist groups. But its targets eventually included even the National Welfare Rights Organization, the National Student Association, the Unitarian Society, and the National Urban League. The IRS finally disbanded the special task force in 1973.

---

[33] ibid., p. 222, affidavit of Johnnie Walters, June 10, 1974.
[34] ibid.
[35] ibid., p. 225, testimony of John Ehrlichman in SSC Executive Session, February 8, 1974.
[36] ibid., p. 239, affidavit of Johnnie Walters, May 6, 1974.

The Central Intelligence Agency does not come off as well as the Justice Department, the FBI, or the IRS. This is in part due to its nature and function as a direct arm of the executive branch, without the kind of statutory protection and definition given to the other agencies, and without the same congressional surveillance.

It is difficult to find the point at which the CIA should have resisted. The request for a wig and for a voice changer would have been difficult to challenge. The White House might have wanted it for a Bebe Rebozo practical joke.

The CIA resistance, when it came, seemed directed more at protecting its own operations and traditions than at turning back administration requests. The CIA may deserve special study as a potentially pure and perfect, self-contained bureaucracy - responsible only to itself and for itself.

The clearest case of resistance involved Deputy Director General Vernon Walters' strong objections to John Dean's suggestion in 1972 that the CIA provide bail and salaries for the Watergate burglars. Walters' argument, as reported, was not altogether based on principle. He argued that falsely implicating the CIA would make the scandal worse and that the CIA had to report any domestic spending to its congressional oversight committees.

General Walters also resisted White House pressure to keep the FBI from investigating what was called "the Mexican connection" of Watergate, a money-hiding or laundering operation of the Committee for the Re-election of the President. The White House wanted the CIA to state or suggest that a CIA operation was involved. CIA resistance was not immediate; initially, the FBI delayed its investigation because Walters followed a Haldeman instruction. Walters, who was new to the CIA at the time, later testified that his response was based on his belief that Haldeman might know something about CIA operations that Walters and Richard Helms, then the CIA Director, did not know. Later, however, after checking with appropriate CIA staff, General Walters told FBI Director L. Patrick Gray that the FBI would not jeopardize any CIA operation by investigating the Mexican matter.

Another instance of CIA resistance is mentioned in the July 1974 Baker report on the CIA. It apparently involved a CIA employee who resisted the CIA's own cover-up.

According to the story, a CIA operative, Lee R. Pennington, Jr., appeared at the residence of James McCord, another Watergate burglar, soon after the Watergate break-in in June 1972 and either destroyed or witnessed the destruction of CIA-related documents. It seems that material about Pennington was removed from the CIA's Watergate files. In February 1974, in response to congressional requests for more information, a statement that the CIA had produced all Watergate-related information for the appropriate congressional committees was prepared for signature by the CIA Director, William Colby. An unnamed personnel-security officer, who was aware of the Pennington matter, made it clear that he could not and would not subscribe to such a statement."[37] This man, according to the Baker report, "was so concerned that the documentary evidence of the Pennington information would be destroyed by others in the CIA that he and a co-employee copied the relevant memoranda and placed them in their respective personal safes."[38] The information subsequently was made available to the appropriate committees and to the Special Prosecutor's office. The same personnel-security officer testified that there had been a CIA meeting in January on whether the Pennington information should be disclosed to the committees and that he told his supervisory CIA personnel: "Up to this time we have never removed, tampered with, obliterated, destroyed, or done anything to any Watergate documents, and we can't be caught in that kind of bind now. We will not do it."[39] (He undoubtedly was not aware that CIA staff in the Executive Office Building had destroyed some receipts for envelopes transmitted from E. Howard Hunt to the CIA. And Richard Helms ordered his tapes destroyed before he left the CIA; he and his secretary later testified that none of the tapes related to Watergate.)

The Baker minority report on the CIA suggested that the CIA ran a cover-up of its own activities similar to that which the White House ran on its operations. It was not clear whether the Agency tried to hide illegal actions or

---

[37] U.S. Senate, Select Committee on Presidential Campaign Activities, minority staff memorandum prepared at request of Senator Howard H. Baker (released July 2, 1974), p. 15.

[38] ibid.

[39] ibid.

only embarrassments. The CIA disputed parts of the Baker report. But it could not escape from the suspicion that its cover-up operations included destroying some evidence, ignoring some congressional requests for evidence, providing summaries instead of some original records that were requested, and possibly even perjury.

Late in 1974 it became apparent that the CIA had covered up far more than activities relating to Watergate. The Agency had spied on domestic organizations opposed to the war in Vietnam, developed files on about 7000 American citizens, and read private mail of American citizens. This is hardly a record to inspire confidence among civil libertarians.

The over-all record establishes how important it is to institutionalize the functions of the most critical agencies of the government - such as the Justice Department, the FBI, the CIA, and the IRS - from political abuse and exploitation. The security and the liberty of citizens should not depend on the chance integrity of governmental employees or the accident of exposure.

A Kind Word for the Military

Today the old saying, "God help the poor sailors on a night like this," has a wider application and should be stated in these words: "God help the military at this time in our history."

The United States military has been operating under the most severe policy handicap, or rather policy vacuum, of any modern military organization.

In the first place, it is misnamed. It is a War Department, involving both offensive and defensive action. Yet it is called the Department of Defense, in keeping with the spirit of the 1928 Kellogg-Briand Pact, which outlawed aggressive wars. There have been only defenders on both sides in all wars since.

There are two things wrong with calling the military the Department of Defense. First, it is dishonest. The sending of Marines to Lebanon by President Eisenhower in 1958 could not by any stretch of military definition be considered defensive action. Nor could President Johnson's intervention in the Dominican Republic in 1965 be considered defensive action. Vietnam, despite all the excuses given for our involvement there, was never vital or necessary to the defense of the United States.

The second thing wrong with using the word "defense" to describe our military department is that it encourages a mentality which is open-ended as to commitment. Our military forces today are charged with the responsibility of defending this country as well as others against all enemies foreign and domestic, present and future, real and imagined - without clear definition of who the enemy is, where he is, or what he is.

When one thinks defensively, the threat or fear always rises to the level of the deterrent and then surpasses it, thus requiring another increase of the deterrent. Thus we moved from atomic bombs to hydrogen bombs, from intercontinental ballistic missiles (ICBMs) to antiballistic missiles (ABMs); from single-delivery systems to multiple independently targeted re-entry vehicles (MIRVs), and so forth.

Under pressures such as these, the Army in 1965 had Douglas Aircraft study what would be required to impose order on the world. The name given the study was "Pax Americana." Later the military started running intelligence checks on political dissidents at home.

A powerful institution like the military inevitably expands into policy vacuums. This was the case in Vietnam, where the military was called upon to act without clear political direction. No military force should be asked to operate in a policy vacuum of this kind or expected, if asked, to achieve any significant success. (This is a situation like that of the clergy who are trying to operate without theology; it is a hard way to go.) Nor should anyone be surprised if under such circumstances military leaders themselves try to develop a policy and influence a President to accept their policy, whatever it may be.

As a rule, since the Korean war, statements of policy and purpose have come only after military commitments and action. Policy seemed to emerge from the military action itself.

In the early years of the Vietnam war (1963-1964), the declared policy was to stabilize the government of South Vietnam. As military commitment increased in 1965, there was an escalation of policy to include preventing invasion from the North. By 1966 our military activities in South Vietnam were of such magnitude that they were said to be directed toward saving all of Southeast Asia from communism and, beyond that, from domination by China. By 1967 the security of the United States, our national honor, and the future of the free world were added to the list. There was not much more to offer after that.

Rather than make political judgments, both President Johnson and President Nixon made military decisions. During the Johnson administration, the public was supposed to be reassured by the knowledge that the President was picking bombing targets. President Johnson, in a television interview after he left office, explained that his decision to limit the bombing and seek peace talks was made after the repulse of the Tet Offensive in early 1968 was assessed as a military triumph for us. This was a clear case of political decision following or depending on a military action.

So, too, most of the Nixon administration decisions with reference to Vietnam were primarily tactical and military. The administration explained "Vietnamization" as a way in which the same things that American troops had been doing would be done by Vietnamese, but with our support. It explained the invasion of Cambodia and Laos in tactical military terms, with scarcely any reference to the political implications.

The principal failures in the war in Vietnam were not military failures. They were failures by civilian leaders of this country to determine policy, to give direction and set limits, to take the diplomatic action necessary to bring the war to an end, and to act responsibly without regard for what such an ending might be called - defeat, surrender, victory, or stalemate.

War should be, if war must be, an extension of politics, as Clausewitz explained. Politics or international policy should not become an extension of war or military power. Yet it has become something very close to that for us, not only in Vietnam but also in other areas of our international concern.

The men who drafted our Constitution did not anticipate the tremendous military power that we now possess. Their concept of the military involved state militia and temporary armies for time of war. Only since 1945 has the United States, outside of wartime, had a military establishment of any size. Now we have a large standing army, a military budget of about ninety-four billion dollars[40], military missions and arms sales all over the world, and significant numbers of troops in Europe and Asia.

None of our institutions or traditions was prepared for this, nor have they adjusted to it in the years since World War II: not the Constitution, not the Congress, not the presidency, not the political parties, not society as a whole, not even the military itself.

The failure of political leaders and institutions created a policy vacuum not just in Vietnam, where it was most evident, but on a much wider scale. This policy vacuum can be filled quite properly and traditionally by having the elected officials of the country determine policy, take responsibility for it, declare it, and attempt to realize it. This is a continuing political need.

It is also a need of the military. Much has been said throughout history about the responsibility of the soldier to the state. A tradition that goes back at least to the Greeks demands his loyalty, commitment to the nation's cause, obedience, and discipline.

Too little has been said about the responsibility of the state to the soldier. This goes beyond the obligation for the soldier's welfare if he is wounded or when he retires. It goes beyond the obligation for the care and support of his dependents. The state has a more fundamental obligation to look to the justice and wisdom of the cause in which the soldier is committed.

A Warning about the Military Establishment

The military-industrial-academic establishment in America has become a kind of republic within the Republic. The military influence, as President Eisenhower warned in his Farewell Address, "is felt in every city, every State house, every office of the Federal government."[41] Since he spoke, the situation has become more serious, more dangerous. The military budget has gone from about forty-five billion to roughly ninety-four billion dollars a year. With military bases and missions in

---

[40] $280.8 billion, FY2000

[41] Public Papers of the Presidents: Dwight D. Eisenhower, 1960-61 (Washington, 1961), p. 1038, farewell address to the American people, January 17, 1961.

many nations of the world, with intelligence operations that include eavesdropping ships and spy satellites, and with sales of several billion dollars' worth of arms around the world, the Defense Department has become perhaps the strongest independent power in world affairs.

Defense Department actions are to a large extent beyond the effective control of the Congress. There is no conspiracy. Rather, the influence of the military in American life is something that happened to us almost without critical judgment and with little evaluation of the process.

The Pentagon spends much of its budget in direct procurement here at home. As the military budget has climbed, the Pentagon has had greater influence upon our foreign policy, upon our domestic policy, and upon the educational institutions of the United States. If it had a significant influence on only one of these, we would have cause for concern; as it has considerable influence on all three, we need to be triply concerned.

Increasing militarization of our foreign policy has been evident in our readiness to respond in military terms to problems around the world which may or may not be susceptible to military solutions. We sponsored an invasion of Cuba in 1961. We intervened, in violation of treaty commitments, by sending troops to the Dominican Republic in 1965. We sent over five hundred thousand troops to Vietnam, sponsored a mercenary army and heavy bombing in Laos, and also intervened in Cambodia.

The tendency to seek military solutions was encouraged by the many contingency plans of the Pentagon and the CIA. When a plan is developed and looks reasonably good, there is always a temptation to try it. This may have been what happened with the Bay of Pigs plan for the invasion of Cuba; it looked so good on paper that somebody said, "Maybe we should give it a try." Or perhaps someone said, "Those fellows over at the CIA and the Pentagon have spent so much time working on this plan, it would be a shame not to use it."

There was also a rumor that the Bay of Pigs plan was prepared in digest form for the Eisenhower administration, which always worked from summaries, and then was speed-read by the Kennedy administration. Under those circumstances it was bound to come up somewhat short, as in fact it did.

Often a plan is largely contingent on an effort by Communists to take over a government somewhere. In the 1965 Dominican Republic crisis, the United States ambassador in that country wired Washington about the trouble, stressing the fact that some Communists were involved in the revolt. A contingency plan was ready. So President Johnson decided that we had to save the country from the Communists and sent in the Marines.

Most serious of all was our involvement in Vietnam. The history of how and why we came to have more than a half-million American troops bogged down in Vietnam is long and complex. Yet if there was one crucial decision that set the course more than any other, it was the decision to commit American troops and try to impose a military solution in a country where the problems are chiefly political and social. The Johnson administration claimed that the real war was "the other war"; it held that the civilian pacification program - or whatever it happened to be called at the moment - was of greatest importance to the outcome of the struggle in Vietnam. But even the pacification program eventually was turned over to the military.

The tendency to look at political problems in military terms was largely responsible for getting us into Vietnam. It was also responsible for much of our difficulty in getting out. Several incidents showed the confusion of roles between the military and the political. In April 1967 the military commander in Vietnam, General William C. Westmoreland, spoke to a joint session of the House and Senate. At that time I questioned on two grounds the appropriateness of having him speak to the Congress. First, it made Congress a captive audience for the presentation of a position on Vietnam which was well known, but which was at the same time highly controversial. Second, it meant using a field commander on active duty to make a case which was political as well as military.

Later in 1967 General Westmoreland returned to the United States and appeared on television with the United States Ambassador to South Vietnam, Ellsworth Bunker, in an attempt to justify the effort in Vietnam. This use of a military commander in what was essentially a public relations capacity was contrary to the tradition of subordination of military to civilian authority, and of military judgment to political judgment, on which this nation was founded.

Early in 1968 the Joint Chiefs of Staff advised President Johnson that the American outpost at Khe Sanh, then besieged by the North Vietnamese, "could and should be defended."[42] The first part of that assurance was a military judgment; the second may have been partly a military judgment, but the context in which it was given was largely political. We ought not to concede a political role to the Joint Chiefs so easily.

As a member of the Senate Foreign Relations Committee, I saw growing evidence of subservience of the State Department and the Johnson administration to determinations and judgments by the military. This observation was sustained by what happened in Vietnam. It was also sustained by the decision to build an antiballistic-missile system, which Robert McNamara and other experts had admitted would add little or nothing to the nation's security.

It was sustained by what happened on arms sales to developing nations. The Johnson administration at times seemed to lobby harder for its arms sales program than for civil rights or aid to education. The Foreign Relations Committee tried to place limits on American arms distribution around the world in 1966 and 1967. Despite administration opposition, we set limits on weapons sales to Africa and Latin America. In opposing these restrictions, the administration claimed that they would seriously hamper our foreign policy in those countries, which, of course, was precisely what we were trying to do.

Administration officials claimed that limits on arms distribution would seriously interfere with military strength in Greece. The Greek colonels, however, seemed more interested in overthrowing their own government than in making a contribution to the North Atlantic Treaty Organization (NATO). The administration said that it needed arms for Iran because of the unsettled situation in the Middle East, and added, "If we do not sell planes to Iran, they will probably go to the Russians for military equipment." We did sell the planes to Iran, and a short

---

[42] statement of the Department of Defense, quoted in *The New York Times*, February 5, 1968, p. 14.

time later the Iranians went to the Russians for additional military equipment anyway.

Arms sales were continued and expanded during the Nixon administration. The United States continued to arm the military dictatorships of Greece and other nations. When India warred with Pakistan in 1971, both sides used arms supplied by the United States. The same thing had happened during their 1965 war. Sales to governments in Latin America increased; this encouraged military coups and border disputes and distracted governments from the economic development needed by their people.

Cash and credit sales of weapons by our government amounted to about one billion dollars in 1968. Ten years later they were over four billion dollars per year. Consequently, both military contractors and American workers are increasingly dependent on arms sales abroad. Senator Robert Dole of Kansas told the Senate in June 1973, "Now, I certainly do not believe the United States should seek to profiteer on the sales of the tools of war around the world. But we should be realistic ..."[43] The Senator argued that aircraft workers in Wichita needed the employment provided by arms sales to other nations.

Much of our representation overseas is military. Apart from our regular troops in Europe and Asia, in 1974 we had about two thousand military agents - including twenty-five generals and admirals - around the world under our military aid programs. We consider very seriously whether we ought to have diplomatic representation in certain countries, and the Senate examines quite thoroughly the qualifications of ambassadors who are sent abroad. Yet the military aid groups, which are sometimes more important, are sent without any kind of formal congressional examination. Without publicity or even public awareness in the United States, these officers carry on missions which have strong political overtones.

The Special Forces, too, are not subject to normal congressional or public supervision. We used to know when the Marines landed and also when they came home. With the Special Forces, we do not know when they go in; we know little about what they do while they are there; and we are never sure about whether they have come home. A variation on this theme has recently been added

---

[43] *Congressional Record*, June 26, 1973, p. S 12084.

in the recent exposure of the fact that the Pentagon contracted with an American corporation to train National Guard troops of Saudi Arabia, which for obvious reasons would like to increase the security in and around its oil fields and pipelines.

In addition to its influence in the international arena, there is serious involvement of the military establishment in domestic affairs of the United States. It is not necessary to accept the old argument that war production stimulates the economy. What is much more significant today is the particular interest developed in certain industries and certain areas of the country with reference to military contracts and other military spending. (The ninety-four billion dollar military budget of the mid-1970s does not represent all costs of military related activities. Other costs include about thirty billion dollars for interest - most of which is interest on debts arising from wars - and over fifteen billion dollars for veterans' benefits.)

What are the effects on our economy of this enormous economic power? Sudden surges within the military sector have certainly contributed to inflation. We still suffer from the inflationary spiral started by deficit spending for the Vietnam war. But this is only one part of the military impact on our economy.

In 1973 the armed forces numbered roughly two million; they were supported by approximately one million civilian workers attached to the Defense Department. Another three to four million civilians were employed in private industry working directly or indirectly to supply the military establishment. This total of roughly seven million people made up about eight per cent of the United States work force. Military technology has become very sophisticated, and its workers are often better paid than workers engaged in other production. Professional workers and skilled blue-collar workers make up a large part of the military employment. Thus military work not only draws away many workers from civilian activities, it also takes a proportionately large number of highly qualified workers.

Entire cities and even states become heavily dependent on military spending - not only for the direct employment it provides but also for the consumer spending and the tax base that it makes available. Decisions to close military bases or to shift contracts to other states always meet strong political opposition and are often postponed or changed for that reason. And new weapons systems such as the B-1 bomber or the Trident submarine are supported by many members of Congress in part because such systems will provide more employment in their districts or states.

Of the weapons systems in general, one might say that it was a great mistake to let the cavalry go. It kept the colonels busy on weekends and kept them from planning war. The cavalry was also cheaper than current weapons systems. Today we have manned bombers instead of a cavalry. The bombers cost a good deal more than the horses.

I was encouraged to learn recently that the army has reactivated a cavalry unit at Fort Hood, Texas. Perhaps we could compete with the Russians in cavalry instead of bombers.

The manned-bomber program since the end of World War II has been the greatest public-works project in the history of the United States, if not of mankind. It has been a significant support for the economy of Washington State during that period. There were B-36s, B-47s, B-50s, B-52s, B-58s, B-70s. Now they are starting all over again with a bomber called the B-1. Besides the manned bombers, we have C-5As, F-111s, ICBMs, MIRVs, and so on. Some members of Congress will vote for almost anything with initials.

When I was in the Senate, I wondered if some of my colleagues would ever feel secure. If the sky were black with bombers, if there were so many nuclear submarines in the ocean that they were running into each other, some senators would still be insecure. I hesitate to mention some of the serious weapons gaps we face, because those senators might introduce legislation to close them. We are way behind the Indians of the Amazon in blowguns and poison darts. In fact, we do not have any poison darts. Moreover, we are short of catapults, crossbows, pikes, shields, cauldrons for boiling oil.

Much of the military sector of the economy consists of research. The federal budget in the 1970s alloted nine billion dollars or so to the Pentagon for research and development. Additional money went to the Atomic Energy Commission for military research.

Military-related industries such as aerospace, electronics, and communications have become a major economic factor. Although the technical competence acquired in these fields can be helpful to the economy, concentration on the military sector has retarded growth in some other areas. Civilian-oriented laboratories and businesses are often unable to match the salaries and equipment that subsidized defense firms offer to scientists and engineers; this handicaps research and development for the civilian economy.

The third area that needs our attention is the influence of the military on education, with tremendous amounts going to colleges and universities in the form of research grants. Through these grants, the military can exercise great influence on science and technology in the United States. They can determine what research shall be carried out. More subtle, but perhaps more important, is the danger that the academic institutions may tailor their whole direction and approach to court the research grants.

University scientists have done research in such areas as chemical and biological warfare, counterinsurgency, missiles, and nuclear bombs. Though student protests have caused some universities to curtail or end their direct participation in such research, many others are still involved. In fiscal 1973, for example, Harvard and Princeton each received about two million dollars for military research; the University of Washington and Columbia University each received four million dollars; the University of California system received twenty-one million dollars; Johns Hopkins University received seventy-five million dollars; the Massachusetts Institute of Technology received one hundred and twenty-three million dollars. Many other universities, both private and public, receive significant sums for military research. Through the research contracts, and also through its Reserve Officers' Training Corps (ROTC) programs, the military influences the whole direction and tone of our national life.

In any society, there should be some institution - and it is hoped there will be more than one - that stands in a position of judgment upon every other kind of institution. This was the role fulfilled by the medieval university in its dedication to the pursuit of knowledge and truth. It is the role the university must continue to fulfill today. It has special importance when the problems which lend themselves to scholarly and academic review are as important to the future welfare of the nation as today's problems are.

I hope that the people will bring some judgment to bear on the direction of the military complex, on the militarization of our foreign policy, and on the influence of the military upon our domestic life. This is particularly important now because America has become a major world leader. We must decide whether we will direct this leadership toward continuing a kind of militaristic policy, or whether we will try to blunt that thrust and inject into American politics and government an understanding of our true role. This nation should not make its record by being a military power, but by demonstrating that all of those things which we claim for ourselves - the right to life, liberty, and the pursuit of happiness and a basic belief in the dignity and worth of the individual - are the real strengths of America and that these are the best gifts we can offer to the rest of the world.

The CIA and the Inner Ring

Though established in 1947 to gather and analyze intelligence, the Central Intelligence Agency has had a significant role in foreign-policy operations. Few people know the full extent of its activities. But there is enough evidence to list the following among the more spectacular:

-Helping oust a Premier of Iran in 1953

-Helping overthrow a President of Guatemala in 1954

-Supporting a U-2 intelligence flight over Russia in 1960, the discovery of which ruined a summit conference

-Sponsoring the Bay of Pigs invasion of Cuba in 1961

-Secretly subsidizing the international activities of many United States education and labor groups for periods ranging up to fifteen years or more

-Directing a mercenary army in Laos in the 1960s and early 1970s

-Engaging in "destabilization" activities which encouraged the overthrow of a President of Chile in 1973

-Plots to assassinate "incompatible" world leaders

-Most recently, domestic spying in the United States.

In some cases the Agency has been charged with doing things without authorization from the executive branch of the government. I do not think this is a very serious problem. Far more serious are the things - such as those listed - which it has done with executive approval.

The defense that everything has been authorized and therefore the CIA should not be criticized is not compelling. If we were to apply this generally, we would have to stop criticizing the President's economic advisers (they would like that), the Secretary of State, and almost every other official of the federal government. But we cannot really blame everything on the President alone.

A serious question must be asked about the methods and instruments used by the CIA. I tried to raise this question once when a new CIA Director was up for confirmation. He declined to reply, citing his legal responsibility "to assure the protection of intelligence sources and methods from unauthorized disclosure."[44] This same defense was used by former CIA Director Richard Helms in a 1975 appearance before a congressional committee.

Some CIA supporters justify questionable methods by saying they are needed to fight communism. This is a modern version of what Oliver Cromwell said when he defended some of his methods: "It's easy to object to the glorious actings of God, if we look too much upon instruments ... Be not offended at the manner; perhaps no other way was left."[45]

If we accept that there is danger everywhere, from communism, or whatever, we develop an unlimited foreign policy and eventually reach a point where we cannot really make distinctions. Our world becomes like that described by Franz Kafka in The Burrow. The little animal of this story had good fortune in hunting; he brought back to his burrow more than he could eat. He stored the surplus but then began to worry about the complications of keeping it all in one place and trying to guard it. The animal thought that perhaps he should scatter it around so that if the enemy came, it would not

---

[44] U.S. Senate, Committee on Armed Services, *Hearings on Nominations of McCone, Korth, and Harlan*, 87th Congress, 2nd session (January 18, 1962), Appendix 1, p. 82, letter of January 19, 1962, from John A. McCone to Senator Richard B. Russell, responding to questions posed by Senator Eugene J. McCarthy.

[45] Oliver Cromwell, The Writings and Speeches of Oliver Cromwell, ed. by William Cortez Abbott (New York, 1970), Vol. II, p. 189, letter of January 1, 1650, to Philip Wharton.

get all the food at once. He built mazes, new tunnels, new chambers - all manner of defenses and deceit - to defend himself and his possessions. Finally he realized that no matter what he did, he could always hear a strange sound. And he feared that the enemy might hear his own sounds, even though he was very careful to be quiet.

The CIA is very careful to be quiet. But it hears strange sounds, and at times its own sounds are also heard.

Another aspect of the Agency was best described by C. S. Lewis in his essay called "The Inner Ring." An Inner Ring is a group whose members are exempt from certain rules that apply to other people. Members of an Inner Ring have a special sense of belonging. Lewis said that an Inner Ring is not necessarily evil in itself. "But the desire which draws us into Inner Rings is another matter. A thing may be morally neutral and yet the desire for that thing may be dangerous.... Of all passions the passion for the Inner Ring is most skillful in making a man who is not yet a very bad man do very bad things."[46]

When this strong human drive has an official function, it may become even more powerful.

The Inner Ring of the CIA - or any intelligence agency - is privileged. Individual responsibility is limited by the oath of loyalty to the agency. Individual conscience is eased by the belief that the goal of the agency is a good one. The anonymity of service in the agency becomes a habit. It is a rejection of name, reward, and recognition. When such self-sacrifice is added to a noble goal, doing the wrong things for the right reasons becomes easier all the time. Finally the process itself may become the end.

Service in the CIA might also be described as a kind of secular monasticism, in that the individual takes a vow of obedience and is then not entirely responsible for his own actions. Though monasticism never relieved the individual of all personal responsibility, the CIA appears to do that for many people.

Other agencies are tempted to escape responsibility by transferring risky work to the secret agency that has immunity. If there are things to be done that the State Department cannot do, they say, "Well, let the CIA do it."

---

[46] C. S. Lewis, "The Inner Ring," in Transposition and Other Addresses (London, 1949), pp. 59 and 62.

Then if something strange happens and members of Congress question it, they can be told, "The CIA did it."

It is as though no one else in the government has political or moral responsibility for what the CIA does, because it is a separate operation with its own special rules. The result of this convenience is that great responsibility is shifted to the CIA, and few people raise the hard questions around the edges.

The Corporations

The corporation is today recognized as a basic force in American life but also as a major problem. It is challenged to answer for its failure to produce enough to meet the needs of the nation. It is challenged for its failure to produce safe and economical products. It is challenged to answer for its waste and its pollution of air, water, and earth. It is challenged for its influence on education, on culture, on politics, and especially on the politics of war.

This examination is long overdue, for the corporation has developed into a separate center of power. It is one which was not anticipated by or provided for in the Constitution. It is one which has not been subject to the general laws dealing with business and, financial practices. And it is one which has assumed functions that go far beyond its original economic purposes.

What we have allowed to develop is a kind of corporate feudalism, one that fits the schoolboy definition of feudalism as a system in which everybody belongs to someone and everyone else belongs to the king. In its modern form, nearly every worker belongs to some corporation. Everyone else - in civil service, on welfare, on workmen's compensation or social security - belongs to the government.

A great corporation might be viewed as a self-contained feudal manor or barony. General Motors, for example, has its own financial institutions, its own distribution system, its own labor policy and social welfare program, its own security system and special investigators, even its own foreign policy. And the foreign policy of ITT in the case of Chile included an effort to have the United States government prevent the election of a certain presidential candidate in that country. Other multinational corporations run their own foreign policies.

I would hesitate to make a direct comparison between today's corporation employees and the serfs of the Middle Ages, yet there are disturbing similarities. Many people become economic captives of the corporations for which they work. Pension programs, family health plans, seniority rewards, vacation and sick leave all limit the freedom of employees to move to other corporations and other types of work. This is true not only of blue-collar workers but also of executives and people in professional fields. I have talked with newspaper people who say, "I can't quit this newspaper and take another job because I would lose my pension program, or my family medical plan. I'm an indentured servant. I'm caught." An indentured servant may be a few steps above a serf, but that is not much consolation.

The loss of freedom that goes with working for a corporation is not always accompanied by security, something that serfs in the Middle Ages did have. Many corporations, particularly those in the military and aerospace industries, stockpiled engineers and other professionals during the boom period of the 1960s. When the corporations faced financial difficulty, or when they no longer needed the professionals, they simply cut them loose to become displaced persons in our society. In recent years, a relief pitcher in the minor leagues has had more security than a Ph.D. in physics who works for a major corporation. And, as the recession deepens, rank-and-file workers are experiencing the same rejection. As of this writing, unemployment, be it permanent or provisional, in the three giant automobile corporations hovers at the rather incredible figure of 20-30 per cent, month after month.

Feudal lords had certain obligations toward the poor, something that cannot be said of our corporations. America's poor and minorities, its undereducated and underfed, are not even the serfs of corporate feudalism. They are its outcasts.

The feudal analogy also holds when one considers the relations between the federal government and large corporations. In case after case of confrontation between the two in the last fifteen to twenty years, the issues have been settled by negotiation. When the question of sending an ambassador to the Vatican was raised in 1960, I suggested that there were other centers of power at which we were unrepresented and which were far ahead of the

Vatican in terms of influence. For example, a President might first send an ambassador to the Pentagon and then to several of the giant corporations: General Motors, du Pont, General Electric, U.S. Steel, some of the oil companies. The relationship was not formalized that way, but negotiation has been the rule.

When du Pont was ordered to divest itself of improperly acquired General Motors stock, existing antitrust laws and penalties were not applied. The Congress passed special legislation to lessen du Pont's economic distress. The company thus avoided the imposition of the law and the attendant corporate stresses, which would have been applied to a smaller corporation under the same circumstances.

Taxation of insurance companies is settled more by negotiation than by public determination. The same was true of the oil-depletion allowance for many years.

Such actions as the award of the TFX airplane contract to General Dynamics in the Kennedy administration and the loan guarantees for Lockheed and Penn Central in the Nixon administration were special concessions to corporate power, political or economic.

The dealings of the government with the steel industry illustrate the feudal character of the corporation-government relationship even more clearly. During the Korean War, President Truman tried to prevent a steel strike by ordering his Secretary of Commerce to take over and operate the steel mills. The case was taken to the Supreme Court, which held that the order was unconstitutional. Subsequent challenges to the industry were handled differently. The Kennedy administration responded to a major price increase not by law or by appeal to courts but by public denunciation, the threat of shifting military purchases to steel companies that had not raised their prices, and even some use of the FBI.

The Johnson administration called presidents of steel companies to the White House for "jaw-boning sessions." The message was that prices should be kept down. It seemed that if the steel executives fixed prices in the White House, it was quite all right, but if they fixed them in Pittsburgh, they might go to jail. It was as though the king had called in the barons and said to them, "If you agree to these things in my presence, they are sanctioned. But if you do it by yourselves in Wales, you are in trouble."

The approach of the Nixon administration to wage-price controls reflected the same feudal character. The idea that it is all right for big government to sit down with big business and big labor to make decisions about the economy is a different concept from what the framers of the Constitution had in mind.

Most of the production in the United States is controlled by corporate management. This is largely a consequence of the special privileges and immunities given by law to corporations to make them more effective in meeting the economic needs of the nation. The grant of special privileges and immunities implied that the corporation provided the best way to produce and distribute goods and also the best way to provide employment.

How then do we explain underproduction and wasteful production in the country? How do we explain the fact that some twenty three million Americans are poor and that over seven million are out of work? Is the explanation to be found in bad corporate management? Are the failures a consequence of outside forces which hamper the corporations in their management of the American economy? Or is the fault in the very concept of the corporation?

The answers are not altogether clear. Undoubtedly some corporations are badly run. Undoubtedly outside policy or forces, such as war and poor fiscal management by government, adversely affect the general economy and specifically affect some industries and areas. More serious, however, than these considerations is the question of whether the concept under which the corporation has developed and operated is a valid one.

I think that the concept of the corporation still has validity but that it must be constantly judged on performance. It is a concept which must prove its own vitality in practice. And if the corporation is to be privileged as it is now, if it is to control most of the forces on which the material well-being of the nation depends, then it must become more effective and more responsible, both socially and economically, than it now is. Its great power must be subject to certain limits.

There are several things we can and must do in the area of corporate reform. First, we must assure greater freedom for corporation employees. As the power of the feudal lords ended, the kings took over. Our problem is to develop systems of security without surrendering personal freedom to the government. One way to give people more freedom is to reduce risk through greater protection in unemployment and health benefits. We need significant improvement in the national unemployment compensation program so that employees will not be as dependent on the unemployment programs of corporations as many now are. We need national health insurance to replace or supplement corporate plans. A recently passed pension reform law sets federal standards for the pension rights of employees; this reform was long overdue. The point is to reduce the economic insecurity of corporation employees while at the same time expanding their personal freedom.

Second, we must make corporations operate within the law. The most obvious laws - the ones with reference to price-fixing and pollution, for example - can and should be enforced. Continued exploitation of migrant workers should not be tolerated. In some cases it can be ended by enforcing existing laws; but where existing legal standards are inadequate, it would be naive to expect even a corporation of some good will to move very far ahead of its competitors.

Third, we must impose upon corporations certain social responsibilities in exchange for their social privileges of limited liability and favorable tax rates.

In considering the concept of social responsibility, it is important not to be distracted by corporate advertising. If we believed the public-relations spokesmen of some corporations, we might think their principal function is charity or the support of education. At one time when I was in Philadelphia, a company was publicizing its provision of free chemicals to kill the termites in the timbers of Independence Hall. You almost had the impression that they did it back in 1776 and that if it had not been for this the Revolution never would have happened. The television ads of some oil companies give the impression that they are refining oil just to provide bird sanctuaries and habitats for small animals. If you drive through Bayonne, New Jersey, you receive a somewhat different impression.

The concept of social responsibility must be related to the corporation's primary economic functions. We have a right to say to the corporations, "We have given you special privileges, and here is what has happened: not

76

enough production, not enough employment, twenty-three million poor."

When full employment does not result from the more or less autonomous operation of the corporations we must consider spreading employment through federal legislation. This can be done by requiring a shorter work day, a shorter work week, or longer vacations. We have not done anything to spread work since the Fair Labor Standards Act of 1938 and the amendments to it established the standard eight-hour day, forty-hour week, and fifty-week year. We have had over thirty years of progress in technology since then - yet the standard for working time remains the same. That Act was a result of the Great Depression and of the need to spread existing work.

Fourth, we should re-examine the political power of corporations. This, of course, is not a new problem. I recall in particular a large corporation in Minnesota. Whenever I was running for Congress on the Democratic-Farmer-Labor ticket, it would give five or six of its employees three months of paid vacation and no instructions. But instead of going to the mountains or the sea, they would always wind up in Republican headquarters.

Serious corruption of principle and practice - not just of individuals - was manifest in corporate influence on the Nixon administration and particularly in illegal contributions to its 1972 re-election campaign.

The time has come to raise a significant challenge to the political, economic, and social power of corporations.

To accept the idea that the corporation, as a center of economic and political power, should be free of social control is to misunderstand the nature of the institution itself. It is also to accept a formula for continued failure to meet the economic and social needs of our country.

The Universities

There is an element of risk in stating what one believes to be the causes of trouble in America, because an explanation is often judged to be approval of what is explained. One can explain a volcanic explosion without being accused of favoring it, but not a riot.

I do not intend to fix blame, but rather to state what I believe have been causes of unrest and protest in universities - without attempting to pass judgment on whether what has happened is disproportionate to the causes. Nor will I say that I sympathize with the ends but disapprove of some of the means. This is an easy way out. Most real problems are, in any case, problems of means.

I do not see the university as a mirror of society. It should be somewhat apart or detached from society.

The university's first responsibility is to transmit the learning of the past - that knowledge which has stood the test of time as truth or which, even though not truth, has had significant bearing on life's own movement and history.

Second, the university has the responsibility to provide an environment for students and scholars so that new knowledge and new ideas can be developed and examined. The medieval concept of the university, expressed in the word studium, was that of an independent body of clerks and scholars set apart from society, called upon to pass a detached judgment on the past and also on the centers of power and influence in society. It was to stand against the church when necessary, against economic institutions, and also against civil authority. The ideal was reflected in physical separation, for early universities were separated from the towns by walls. The Harvard Yard reflects this same concept.

The university has a third responsibility as an agent of social change and an institution of a free society. It can perform this function either directly or indirectly: sometimes by going out to society, and sometimes because outside forces intrude and demand attention. New disciplines in the field of social studies make this involvement immediate and continuing.

The free university is more abstraction than reality. This certainly is true of universities and colleges in the United States. Most of our early schools were established not as free and independent institutions but as instruments of defined and limited purpose. Many were organized to defend and advance a particular kind of Christianity. Their religious detachment, where it exists, has been a gradual development.

State support of higher education in the second half of the nineteenth century was not designed to develop free universities, but to create institutions which would serve society in a practical way. Some colleges and universities, and many departments within others, were set up as an extension of the business community. Special chairs, if not whole departments, were often established through grants and foundation support as an extension of individuals.

There have been three outside forces bearing on university life in recent years.

One was the war in Vietnam, which demanded a practical judgment within the context of history and also a moral judgment with regard to individual commitment. The first judgment was demanded of students because they were students. The second was required because they were citizens, but more immediately because they were called upon to make the moral decision of whether they would be involved in war, whether they would commit their time and lives.

The second outside force was - and is - racial injustice in America. The response to this on campuses has two aspects, as did the response to the war. First is a detached one, which is required of students as they try to pass an academic judgment on the racial problems of the United States. Second is a personal and moral one, involving discrimination on campus - where it exists - and beyond that a judgment on what one should do about discrimination or exploitation elsewhere.

The third outside force is concern over process or participation, over freedom and dependence, over the institutionalization of life and freedom within a social structure. This bears upon the nation's political life, the problem of corporate power, and the internal problems of the university itself.

No one should be surprised that these forces have run so strongly on university campuses, nor surprised that protest has been manifest against the ROTC, military and business recruitment on campus, racial discrimination on campus, and outdated methods of education.

Nor should we be surprised at the slowness of response. The university was a projection of the elementary and then the secondary schools in this country. This is the reverse of the situation in other times, in other places. Many countries had the university but no primary and secondary schools. Great universities of the Middle Ages and the Renaissance flourished independently of any preparatory schools; preparatory schools simply did not

79

exist. The gradual growth of American universities from lower school systems continued our concept of the student as child and the institution as acting in loco parentis. In my view this was a great mistake as to what the university should be.

Another source of the problem of response may lie in an inherent attitude of American culture: that no one exists unless he or she is producing material goods. The consequence of this is that young people who in another time would have been writing the Declaration of Independence, governing communities, running businesses, debating the concepts of an emerging nation - as they were in the time of the American Revolution - are today students and thus looked upon and treated as grown children.

The Vietnam war has ended. Racial injustice has been reduced, though more progress is needed.

We must continue to seek changes in higher education itself.

But of special concern to me, both for the university and for society, are some of the underlying concepts that run through education and through culture in this country.

The first half of this century was marked by false optimism. It was generally held that through the advance of science, improved communication, and new political forms, all the ancient evils that had afflicted mankind would soon become matters of purely historical significance. Many believed that there would be an end to ignorance and poverty and poor health and tyranny, that the machine would permit man to develop all of his higher faculties and powers - those that are unique to him in creative thought and goodness and in the expression of art. People hoped and believed that, freed from spending most of their time and energy in making a living, they could build a society in which they would be free to be themselves.

We know now that science and technology have a tremendous potential for exploitation and also contain seeds of destruction, that the new political forms are subject to new forms of demagoguery, and that mass communication can pervert as well as educate. The tyranny of any one of these is as bad as the tyranny of a despot.

We know that the machine, instead of being the servant of man, can in fact become his master. And we know that in making material production and consumption the center of human activity, we have profoundly changed the framework wherein we determine our values, if we have not changed the values themselves.

We have begun to accept the principle that one ought to do what it is technically possible to do. As Erich Fromm has ironically observed, "If it is possible to build nuclear weapons, they must be built even if they might destroy us all. If it is possible to travel to the moon or to the planets, it must be done, even if at the expense of many unfulfilled needs here on earth..."[47] This kind of technical progress, in a sense uncontrolled and not subject to truly rational direction, threatens to become the source of values in itself. The program itself can become the purpose, and power itself set the objectives for our society.

Fromm says that we have accepted a principle of maximal efficiency and output. This results in a coordinate principle of minimal individuality. "The social machine works more efficiently, so it is believed, if individuals are cut down to purely quantifiable units whose personalities can be expressed on punched cards..."[48]

What then becomes of man in this process?

Totally concerned with production or with sale and consumption of things, Fromm says, he becomes more and more like a thing himself. He tends to become a total consumer, engaged in the passive taking - in of everything from cigarettes to liquor to television to movies and even to lectures on books and poetry. His thinking or his being then becomes split from his emotions, his truth from any kind of commitment, and his mind from his heart. This spirit begins to affect the whole social structure. Things and achievements that are measurable become more important and attractive than life and growth itself.

The university is somewhat at fault here. Much of recent thought and education has been within a pattern of determinist ideas and determinist processes, both of which deny individual freedom and responsibility.

This determinism has been reflected in three general themes or academic currents: one, evolution; two, psychoanalysis; and three, a positivist and determinist

---

[47] Erich Fromm, The Revolution of Hope (New York, 1968), p. 32.
[48] ibid.

acceptance of process, incorporating Auguste Comte's "sociological law," in which laws and not causes explain social and historical change. It is all too easy to give the appearance of wisdom and to avoid responsibility by saying, "We must have evolution, not revolution."

The generalized application of the theory of evolution to man is a limiting and reductive force. The fact is that evolution itself has had less effect upon life in this century than in any century, for life has certainly come under more rational control, for good or bad, in recent years than ever in the past.

The second limiting force in modern education and scholarship and culture is psychoanalysis. I do not question the knowledge that has come from psychoanalysis, but protest the oversimplification that has come with it, the exaggerated claims that have been made for it, and the loss of freedom that goes with uncritical acceptance and application of its theory and its vocabulary. I propose a challenge to those who suggest that the course of human events has been, and can be, very clearly changed by the interpretation of dreams and the concept of the superego, the ego, and the id. I prefer to declare for those young people today who would rather be held responsible for their actions than have them explained away as arising from the unconscious or the subconscious.

The third form of determinism that runs through our culture is more subtle and difficult to define. It is not as simple as Marxist determinism. If it were, it would be easy to define and to clarify (even though Marxism, in some of its forms, is not as antihumanist or as determinist as it is sometimes said to be). The determinism of which I speak is the determinism of process or of procedure the uncritical acceptance of certain ideas, the uncritical yielding to procedures.

The clearest example of this today is the militarization of American government policy, culture, and thought.

Military language has invaded the area of civilian politics. Efforts to deal with domestic problems have been described in such terms as "war on poverty," war on ignorance," and "war on cancer" - a slight change from the "crusades" of the Eisenhower administration. Yet these problems cannot even be understood in the terminology of war. Poverty does not yield to the instrumentalities of war or to the psychology of war. Ignorance cannot be reduced by the techniques of war.

The individual in America is caught up not only in the military complex but in a whole combination of complexes.

The universities and colleges have also been involved. They have sent men to Washington with theoretical books they had written like Walt Rostow and The Stages of Economic Growth - who then acted as if their mission were to prove their theory right. The universities may be faulted for not running up the warning flags much earlier than they did. The interests of their scholars seemed to lie more in analyzing what happened and explaining how things operated - in seeking determinist laws of behavior where no laws could be found - than in making objective judgments on the likely consequences of policy decisions and on whether things should be permitted to go on as they were.

Universities in recent years have been in trouble that is to a large extent of their own making. It is not enough for them to assert their independence in absolute fashion. The real charge to the universities is to reconstitute themselves as centers of normative, purposeful, and critical thought, free from pressures of factions - political, religious, and economic - and free, insofar as possible, from identified errors of the past.

The university must be prepared to run some of the risks Socrates ran in the pursuit of truth. Its role is essentially to walk through the Red Sea dry-shod, if that is possible, opening the waters at the right time and allowing them to close also at the right time; to analyze and to synthesize; to be impersonal and detached, and at the same time to open the way to commitment; to recognize that at all times those with whom it deals - students, faculty, administrators, even trustees - must be treated as persons.

And having made one passage, it may be called upon to make another.

The Democratic and Republican Parties

After the 1964 defeat of the Republican presidential candidate, Senator Barry Goldwater, political pundits started writing about the end of the Republican party as an effective political instrument.

Lyndon Johnson defeated Goldwater in 1964 by a margin of about sixteen million votes. Four years later that margin disappeared; Republican candidate Richard Nixon won the presidency by roughly five hundred thousand votes. And four years after that the same Richard Nixon, running for re-election, defeated the Democratic candidate, Senator George McGovern, by a margin of almost eighteen million votes.

One must ask whether presidential elections depend principally on the personalities of candidates, whether the country changed that much politically in a period of only eight years, or whether the political parties changed that much.

If one concludes that personality is the dominant factor, the party search between elections should be for the right man or woman. Yet in the elections since the death of Franklin D. Roosevelt, with the exception of the choice of Dwight Eisenhower in 1952 and 1956, personality does not appear to have been the principal force in determining the outcome. If it were, one would have to believe that John Kennedy's margin over Richard Nixon in 1960 would have been larger and also believe that Nixon's margin over McGovern in 1972 would have been smaller.

Undoubtedly the country changed in eight years, but not enough to explain the voting swing from 1964 to 1972. This leaves only the political parties as possible causes of the swing.

What happened to the Republican party? Certainly its leader, President Nixon, made significant changes in his past positions. Despite his long support of the cold war, by 1972 he took credit for a major opening to Mainland China and for improved relations with Russia. Though representing a party that used to denounce Democratic administrations for deficit spending, by 1972 President Nixon defended his own deficits. He had become a Keynesian.

Undoubtedly these switches drew some votes to Mr. Nixon in 1972. But the Republican party remained then - and remains now - essentially what it has been for some twenty years. It draws its strength principally from the business and management class - from the captains of industry and finance, the businessmen of the large cities, and the small businessmen of small towns. The party also draws support from professionals and semiprofessionals and from salesmen and clerical workers who identify with the hopes and fears of management.

Some observers divide the Republicans into regulars and liberals, but I am not persuaded that these labels have great significance. The regulars are like men standing on the shore while someone drowns: they advise him to take deep breaths of fresh air if he wishes to be saved. The liberals go one step further: if a man is drowning forty feet from shore, they throw him a twenty-five-foot rope and say that they have gone more than halfway.

In any case, there was not enough that was new or different in the Republican appeal of 1972 to explain the wide margin of victory. Nor can the sabotage of Democratic campaigns alone explain the wide margin. The explanation must lie chiefly in the failure of the Democratic party.

Senator George McGovern must take much responsibility for things such as the Eagleton affair, the thousand-dollars-per-person income-distribution proposal, and the way that the case for cutting the military budget was presented. Each of these had some bearing on the outcome of the election. But the fact that these mistakes could be made and were made must in large part be attributed to the weaknesses and failures of the Democratic party itself.

During the Franklin D. Roosevelt era, the Democratic party welded together many diverse elements into an effective majority. This majority was able to win elections and was also able to govern the country. The Democratic party included millions in the North and in the South. It included Catholics in the large cities and Protestants in rural areas. It included the most ardent advocates of civil rights and the strongest segregationists. It had workers and farmers and others whose economic interests were often in conflict.

Yet the Democratic party in power was able to move freely on most issues of national and international policy. A minority satisfied that its special needs were being met was less likely to be critical of party action on other issues. In the period of the New Deal, Southern Democrats in Congress, who were chiefly interested in agricultural problems, supported such things as social security and national labor legislation. The general appeal was for minorities to work together so that the problems of each might in some measure be met.

Democrats followed the old formula with less and less success after World War II - long after the economic, social, and political realities had changed.

President Harry S. Truman put the old combination together in 1948, with the exception of the South, much of which defected on the civil rights issue. Truman won by the narrowest of margins, but his victory in essence signaled the demise of Roosevelt's old "unbeatable" combination.

It did not work for the Democrats in 1952 or in 1956, against a nonpolitical candidate, Dwight Eisenhower.

John Kennedy made the same appeal in 1960, adding an emphasis on strengthening the military and an appeal to the independent vote of suburban professionals and semiprofessionals. He was barely able to defeat Richard Nixon.

The 1964 election was outside of any political context: it was influenced significantly by the assassination of President Kennedy. It was also influenced by Senator Goldwater, who asked the electorate to vote against history - an appeal which never draws much support.

In 1968 Hubert Humphrey tried but could not put the old combination together.

The Democratic party should have recognized, at least after 1960, that it could not safely rely on a conglomerate of minority interests as the way to victory. Some of those interests no longer had great political significance. In the case of others, ground had been lost to the Republicans.

In the earlier campaigns the Democrats could stress the minority issues and at the same time advocate policies of broad national and international significance. But it had become increasingly clear by the 1960s that the emphasis had to be placed on broad national and international policies, while the special problems of minorities received supplemental attention.

The Democrats were called upon to make the choice of being simply a majority party in polls and registration and in control of Congress or of again becoming an effective governing majority and a presidential party.

In 1968 the Democrats refused to make this choice. At the Chicago convention of that year, the party rejected the support of potentially one third of its voters - those who opposed the war and who had raised new political issues - and dug in with the old guard and the old methods.

In 1972 those who had been rejected at the Chicago convention rallied behind Senator George McGovern. With the help of new rules and procedures, they controlled a convention and a campaign which effectively alienated one third or more of the traditional Democratic voters. Whereas those who controlled in 1972 were more sophisticated and less physical than those who ran the 1968 convention, their methods were essentially the same. When the party rules were more useful than the law, the rules were applied, as in the rejection of Mayor Richard Daley's delegation. When the law was advantageous, as in the issue of sharing the California delegation, the law was applied. So the defeat of 1972 was not at all surprising.

The problem of putting the Democratic party back together is not as easy as that of the Republicans after 1964. The Goldwater break was more in the nature of a personal, almost physical, aberration. It was not ideological or organic. The difference between the supporters of Goldwater and those who opposed him was essentially one of degree. Reconciliation after such a break is relatively easy.

In the case of the Democrats, the problem involves historical claims to the party and traditional practices. It involves structural and procedural changes never seriously at issue among the Republicans. It involves hard judgments on whether the emphasis should be on party strength and party position, or whether the party should seek to personalize and to incarnate its conflicts and contradictions.

If the Democrats are to justify their claim to being the party of progress, innovation, and challenge, they will have to come up with more than age, sex, race, or other physical standards for the selection of delegates. The Democratic party must so reorder its operations, set its policies and programs, and choose its candidates as to give the voters of the country a clearer choice than it offered in 1968 and a more relevant one than it offered in 1972. Otherwise, it will fail as it did in 1968 and 1972. A party that has lost twice to Richard M. "Nixon should be subjected to thorough re-examination.

Alternatives to the Major Parties

Dissatisfaction with the two major parties is widespread in the United States. This dissatisfaction is not regional or sectional. It is not restricted to one economic or cultural group, but is based on frustration and disappointment which have a historical base.

In the case of the Republican party it began in 1964, when many liberal or moderate Republicans, believing that their position was not recognized or represented in the party's choice of Senator Barry Goldwater, refused to support his candidacy. The nomination of Richard Nixon in 1968 did not wholly allay their doubts about their party. More recently, the Watergate affair and other scandals of the Nixon administration alienated conservative Republicans, as well as the liberals and the moderates. (It is distressing to hear some people say that the final outcome of Watergate proved that the system works. That is like saying that the crossing of the Atlantic by the Titanic was a great success because some people survived. Not all the lifeboats sank - just the ship.)

Many Democrats experienced frustration in 1968, when candidates and proposals of antiwar Democrats were rejected in Chicago and supporters of those candidates and proposals were beaten and abused in the convention hall, in the Conrad Hilton hotel, and on the streets of Chicago.

One of the slogans of the Goldwater campaign of 1964 was, "A choice, not an echo." A cynical observation on the 1968 campaign was, "Not a choice, but two echoes." Reflecting this unhappiness over the lack of choice, many people were involved in efforts to run a third or fourth candidate in 1968.

In 1972 many traditional Democrats were unhappy with the nomination of Senator George McGovern and with the conduct of his campaign. Many other voters were unhappy with both candidates, as was shown by the fact that the voter turnout was the lowest in over twenty years.

Yet there are real obstacles to a third party or independent campaign in the United States. First, party loyalty is still a real force in American politics. The older voters become, the more they have voted for one party, and the greater their commitment to that party is likely to be. Party activists and officials develop even stronger loyalties.

In addition to loyalty and commitment, there is a traditional argument for the two-party system. Throughout most of our history, political action has been centered in two major parties. The working of the two-party system has been a matter of some pride to us. We have been quick to assert that a two-party system makes democracy work, whereas a multiparty system, such as that used in some European countries, is not conducive to good democratic government.

The idea of two-party democracy has been accepted as the mark of political maturity and responsibility, to the point where a challenge to such a system is looked upon as almost heretical. Yet the system certainly shows signs of weakness today.

Party loyalty is declining. More and more persons, when asked to give their party designation, call themselves independents. Many others, who still call themselves either Democrats or Republicans, do not have the kind of loyalty that once marked party membership.

A 1974 Gallup poll showed that 34 per cent of American voters considered themselves independents. The Republican party was claimed by only 24 per cent. The Democratic party had more strength but could not find too much to cheer about in the Gallup poll. It had gone from 42 per cent in 1940 to a high of 53 per cent in 1964, then back down to 42 per cent in 1974.

A 1973 Harris poll showed somewhat different figures, with a smaller percentage of independents and a larger percentage of Democrats. But it showed a significant gain in independent strength, not only among the population as a whole but also among important groups. It showed union members going from 17 per cent independents in 1968 to 26 per cent independents in 1973, small town residents going from 16 per cent to 28 per cent independents in those years, and voters in the $10,000-$15,000 income group going from 12 per cent to 28 per cent independents in the same period. Evidently many voters are dissatisfied with both the major parties.

College students, a significant force in American political life, are even more inclined to be independents than other groups. A Gallup poll in 1974 showed that 49 per cent of the college students regarded themselves as independents.

A 1972 survey by the University of Michigan's Institute for Social Research found that black citizens - long a mainstay of the Democratic coalition - were also more inclined to be independents than previously. The survey found that black identification with the Democratic party had dropped from 85 per cent in 1968 to 69 per cent in 1972, and that most of the non-Democrats identified themselves as independents. Black voters have supported several third parties or quasi-parties in the past ten years, such as the Mississippi Freedom Democratic party, the National Democratic party of Alabama, the United Citizens' party in South Carolina, and the D.C. Statehood party in the nation's capital.

The theoretical argument for the two-party system is also subject to challenge. A two-party system may be a device that makes immature democracy work, but it is less necessary in a mature democracy; that is, one with more democratic procedures and a better-informed electorate. The two-party system can be defended only if the parties themselves are responsive to the needs of the country and if they give the people a choice on major issues affecting the country.

In fact, a coalition might result in better government. For example, had the choice of a President been thrown into the House of Representatives in 1968, the House might have made as good a choice as that made by the minority of voters who elected Richard Nixon. A formal and identifiable coalition in the House and Senate might work better than the floating coalitions which now mark the Congress. Theoretical arguments aside, however, the fact is that the two-party tradition is not as strong in the United States as it has been made out to be. It has been challenged regularly through the years. In the election of 1796, for example, there were thirteen candidates for the presidency. Five were Federalists, three Democratic-Republicans, one Anti-Federalist, three Independent Federalists, and one Independent.

Most of the political contests during the early 1800s were among factions within the Democratic-Republican party. But Andrew Jackson and his policies in the 1830s stirred up criticism and brought about party opposition in what became the Whig coalition. This set the stage for the splinter-party movements that followed.

After 1840 there were splinter parties in almost every election. Most are remembered for lost causes such as free silver, greenbacks, and the single tax. But some are credited with developing important policy positions on such things as regulation of the railroads, opposition to monopolies, and establishment of price supports for agriculture.

In addition to their indirect influence, splinter parties have sometimes had more obvious and measurable success.

In 1848 Zachary Taylor, a Whig, won over Lewis Cass, a Democrat, while Martin Van Buren, running on the Free-Soil ticket, drew 10 per cent of the vote. Nine Free-Soilers were elected to the House of Representatives, and two were sent to the Senate. In the House, where neither the Whigs nor the Democrats held a majority, the Free-Soilers held the balance of power in the next Congress.

By 1856 the Free-Soil movement had disintegrated and a new third party - the Republican party - had been born. In that year James Buchanan, a Democrat with roughly 46 per cent of the vote, defeated John C. Fremont, a Republican who received 33 per cent, and also Millard Fillmore, who ran as the American-party (Know-Nothing) candidate and received 21 per cent of the vote.

The main issue of the Republicans was that of keeping slavery out of the territory then being opened for settlement. The Republican party included all-out abolitionists, Free-Soilers, Independent Democrats, Conscience Whigs, Know-Nothings, Barnburners, and Prohibitionists. But more important than the issues was the cultural cohesiveness of the party. The Republican party was then made up principally of "Yankees" in New England and in the northern half of the United States to the west, the population of which at that time consisted largely of those who had moved from the New England states.

In 1860, within ten years after it was founded, the Republican party, with roughly 40 per cent of the popular vote in a four-way contest, won enough electoral votes to make Abraham Lincoln President of the United States. This was quick success for the new party, which went on to dominate the politics of the Midwest until well into the twentieth century.

Other third-party or splinter-party movements were not as successful as the Republican party. Between 1872 and 1936, however, the splinter-party vote was a significant negative influence in presidential elections, particularly in the West. During those years, nearly all the Western and many Midwestern states were delicately balanced between the two major parties. As those states switched from side to side, they generally switched together and helped choose many Presidents.

Third parties have long been successful in electing members of the Congress. A high point of third-party representation was in the 1850s, when the American party (Know-Nothings) in one Congress had forty-three members of the House of Representatives. This was at a time when the total membership of the House was only two hundred and thirty-four. In the late 1890s the Populists, Fusionists, and Silverites together had at least twenty members of the House and seven members of the Senate.

The high point for third-party representation in the twentieth century was in 1937, when the Congress had sixteen members who were neither Republicans nor Democrats; they were a mixture of Progressives and Farmer-Laborites.

The record of third parties in presidential politics in the twentieth century is one of mixed success. The campaign of Theodore Roosevelt in 1912 was outside the usual context of a third-party movement; that is, it was not a real third-party effort. It was not regional. It was not based upon ideological differences within the Republican party, nor was it carried on as an educational program. It simply sought victory for Theodore Roosevelt. Woodrow Wilson was elected in 1912 with almost 42 per cent of the popular vote. But Teddy Roosevelt received 27 per cent of the vote, which was a higher percentage than the regular Republican candidate received in that year. Roosevelt was credited or blamed for the outcome of that election.

In 1924 Senator Robert M. La Follette, Sr., of Wisconsin ran as an independent candidate for President. Despite a late start and poor financing, he won almost 17 per cent of the popular vote.

Since the end of World War 11, the only splinter parties to win electoral votes have been based in the South. In 1948 Strom Thurmond's States' Rights (or Dixiecrat) party received 2.4 per cent of the vote and thirty-nine electoral votes. In the same year, Henry Wallace, the candidate of the Progressive party, won about 2.4 per cent of the popular vote but no electoral votes. George Wallace, running in 1968 for the American Independent party, carried five Southern states, drew 13.5 per cent of the national popular vote, and won forty-six electoral votes. Wallace was strong enough to keep both

Nixon and Humphrey from winning clear majorities in twenty-five states.

The discontent in the country could well manifest itself in a successful independent or third-party effort in the near future.

The alternative is to surrender the United States indefinitely to the Democrats and Republicans - to let them just take turns running the country. On the record, they have not done very well by the country in recent years.

The two-party system is not a matter of revelation. It was not written on the back of the tablets that Moses brought down from the mountain. It was not even recommended by the very wise, even inspired, men who drafted our Constitution. It does not have an unbroken tradition. So on all counts - revelation and wisdom and Constitution and experience it is subject to rather serious challenge.

Part II Operations

A Hard Look at the Primaries

The Democratic primary campaigns of 1972 were expensive and exhausting and to say the least - or the most - inconclusive on issues. They were a significant force in choosing the Democratic nominee, Senator George McGovern. They also showed that the Democratic party was greatly divided, if not confused, and that it would have difficulty in uniting behind the nominee.

The 1972 primaries, did little to clarify the issues. In Florida and Michigan the race was principally for the school board (busing issue), and in Wisconsin for county or city assessor (property tax). Only in California was there a clear confrontation on the military-spending issue. The problem of welfare reform was not adequately debated in any of the primaries.

This is not to fault the primary system itself. If there had been no primaries in 1972 and if instead there had been precinct caucuses followed by county and state conventions in all the states, the picture might have been just as clouded.

Yet it is difficult to demonstrate that Democratic presidential primaries over the last twenty-five years have had many positive results either in determination of issues or in selection of candidates.

One exception was 1960, the year in which Senator John Kennedy established himself as a candidate through victories over Senator Hubert Humphrey in the Wisconsin and the West Virginia primaries and then went on to win the nomination and the November election. There is no solid reason, however, to believe that the primaries apart from the person determined the political events of that year or to believe that Senator Humphrey, had he won the same early primaries, would have been nominated.

In 1952 Senator Estes Kefauver challenged President Harry S. Truman in early primaries. Shortly after Kefauver won the New Hampshire primary, Truman announced that he would not run again. Senator Kefauver then went on to win eleven more primaries. Yet he was not nominated. Again in 1956 he won nine primaries, while Adlai Stevenson won seven primaries and the Democratic nomination. Kefauver was the vice-presidential candidate that year, but he did not receive the lesser nomination as a gift because of his primary showing. He won the nomination in the convention when Stevenson opened the choice of vice-presidential candidate to the delegates.

In 1964 there were no significant primary challenges. In 1968 there were. In that year President Lyndon Johnson, after a mixed decision in the New Hampshire primary, after Senator Robert Kennedy had declared his candidacy, and two days before the Wisconsin primary (which Johnson subsequently lost by a margin of about 21 per cent) announced that he would not be a candidate for re-election.

What might have happened if Senator Kennedy had not been assassinated or if President Johnson had not withdrawn, no one can know. At the Chicago convention in August of that year, the Democratic party chose to reject the primary results as to both candidate and the issue of the Vietnam war. The convention chose Vice President Hubert Humphrey, who had competed in only two primaries and had lost both and whose support came principally from states that had not held primaries. This support was supplemented by delegates from states such as Indiana and Nebraska, which after the death of Senator Kennedy chose to ignore what the primaries had indicated.

What then is to be said for primaries? Are they an expensive political side show that does little more than fill the gap between the end of the winter-sports season and the time when the baseball season becomes serious? Do they contribute anything really worthwhile to the political process, or would they if they were conducted in some other way?

I have no certain answers. Minnesota adopted a presidential primary designed to make Harold Stassen a front runner, at least for a short time. The primary law was repealed after two bad experiences - that is, bad in the judgment of party leaders. One was Dwight Eisenhower's near defeat of Stassen in the 1952 primary. The second was Kefauver's defeat of Adlai Stevenson in the 1956 primary, despite the fact that Stevenson had been the Democratic nominee in 1952 and had in 1956 the full support of the party organization, the endorsement of Senator Hubert Humphrey, and the endorsement of Governor Orville Freeman.

What has happened since in Minnesota neither proves nor disproves that abolition of the primary was good. The Republican party in convention was bitterly divided over the Goldwater choice in 1964, and there was sharp division over my candidacy and that of Mr. Humphrey in 1968. In 1972 President Nixon faced no serious opposition on the Republican side. But Senator Humphrey was sharply challenged by a liberal/peace coalition that made significant gains in the precinct caucuses and later in the state convention.

One or two things do seem clear about primaries.

The records of 1952 and 1968 indicate that an incumbent President who is successfully challenged in primaries is, either for political or for personal reasons, not likely to run for re-election.

Primaries have also eliminated some candidates early in the political year or at least before the national conventions: Stassen, for example, in 1948 when he was done in by Thomas Dewey in Oregon, and Senator Edmund Muskie after poor showings in several of the early primaries in 1972. Sometimes, however, a candidate is only sorely wounded in an early primary. He may say, as did the hero of an old English ballad, that he will lie down and bleed awhile, then rise and fight again.

Whether it is good to have candidates eliminated early along the campaign trail is not certain, unless the objective is simply elimination and the nomination is to go to the one who survives - a kind of political trial by ordeal.

When primaries have not proved much about candidates, what have they done about the issues? In 1948 there was no real test in Democratic primaries on the civil rights issue. That test came at the convention itself. In

1960, a year when primaries did have considerable bearing on the selection of the Democratic candidate, there was no significant division among Democrats on the issues. The Republican primaries of 1964 presented a clear choice on issues as personified in the candidacies of Senator Barry Goldwater and Governor Nelson Rockefeller.

In 1968 the primary test in the Democratic party was on the issue of the Vietnam war. Though the results were conclusive, the party in convention chose to ignore them. In 1972 the Democratic primaries had some bearing on issues, though any of the major candidates except Governor George Wallace could have run on the platform that emerged from the national convention. The Republican primaries of 1972 were marked by the inability of insurgents (Representative John Ashbrook on the right and Representative Paul McCloskey on the left) to mobilize support against the policies of President Nixon.

Despite the fact that little positive good can be attributed to the primaries as a way of choosing presidential candidates or formulating platforms, it does not automatically follow that they should be eliminated. Neither does it follow that there should be more primaries or that there should be a national primary.

The idea of a national primary is the worst of all proposals. Senators Mike Mansfield and George Aiken, after one of their regular Senate Restaurant breakfasts, made such a proposal. A national primary would at most quantify the failures and inadequacies of current primary practices. It would be difficult to administer, would certainly require a series of runoffs, and would probably cost more than the present primaries. Since there could be no selection of primaries on the part of candidates, it would give even greater advantage to candidates who have private fortunes or large financial backing.

A national primary would discourage state political organization and activities. It would encourage the proliferation of political parties for the wrong reason, since the easier way might well be to run under a new party banner rather than to make the effort required in a national primary. It would probably result in the formation of essentially the same substructure of politics that now goes into national elections. There would certainly be caucuses to support candidates and possibly primaries to choose primary candidates. The last state of politics might be worse than the first.

The ways of democracy are not simple, clear, and direct. William Stafford, a poet from Kansas, has warned that "if we purify the pond, the lilies die."[49]

What one proposes to do about primaries depends in large measure on what one conceives to be the role of major parties in American politics.

I believe that primaries should not be an instrument for the capture of a party by a faction or by individuals for personal use or for aims not generally consistent with the party tradition. A political party, as Woodrow Wilson wrote, should not be an organization to be taken over and used but an organism alive to issues and people. Thus, although the liberal Republicans did not have a right to take over the Republican party in 1964, they did not deserve the Goldwater candidacy, which was retrogressive and counter to new forces in the Republican party. In the same way, the Democrats should not have been forced in 1968 to support a military policy in Vietnam that contradicted the party's tradition in foreign policy.

The primary could become an effective means for clarifying party positions and choosing candidates. At some point in the process of choosing presidential candidates and determining party platforms, there should be a break in the straight-line, popular, arithmetical choice. Persons and party must be made responsible to the public. This was the principle incorporated in the electoral college provided by the Constitution. Responsible persons were to be chosen as presidential electors. They, in turn, were to make responsible selections and be held answerable to their constituencies. This principle, I believe, is sound and should be the basis of primary laws as it is the basis of proceedings in convention states.

Among existing primaries, the New York primary comes closest to conforming. In that primary, the names of presidential candidates are not on the ballot. The delegate's name alone is formally taken to the voters for judgment. The delegate or his candidate must inform the public who the delegate is, if that is necessary, or whom he supports, if that is necessary. The delegates once chosen are not legally committed to any candidate,

---

[49] William Stafford, "Connections," in West of Your City (Los Gatos, Calif., 1960), p. 52.

although they may have personal and moral commitments. The delegates go on to the national convention, at which candidates are chosen and the platform is written.

This procedure conforms to the electoral-college procedures of the Constitution and to the caucus system where the caucuses are open and democratic. It also opens the way to greater participation by voters, since it does not require their physical presence at caucuses. It can offset the imbalance that often arises in caucuses because of the physical effort of some factions or persons to get their supporters to the caucuses. Consequently, it may result in more democratic participation.

This kind of primary could test the wider use of absentee balloting and the spreading of voting time over several days, experiments which might then be used as bases for changing voting practices in general elections.

Laws which favor existing parties and which tend to underwrite the two-party system should be challenged on constitutional grounds. One kind of discrimination is the requirement in several states that independent efforts and new parties must file their petitions for electors much earlier than the two major parties name their electors. Moreover, by 1972 six states and the District of Columbia had no statutory provision for independent electors. Three states barred independent electors altogether. This seems to defy the intent of the founding fathers in writing the electoral-college provisions.

The way must be kept open to outside challenge from new political movements.

During our colonial period, James Otis protested the tyranny of taxation without representation. Unrepresentative politics, which leads to unrepresentative government, may not be tyranny, but it is certainly not the strength of democracy.

Personality Cuts

In the British parliamentary system, the Prime Minister generally represents the office and the party first his personality is secondary. Harold Wilson, for example, is a very proper representative of the Labour party. He is its leader, but he is not an incarnation of the party.

The United States, on the other band, developed a cult of the person in the presidency. This was true of Franklin

D. Roosevelt and later of John Kennedy and Lyndon Johnson. Many Americans seemed to accept the idea that the President was bigger than life and somehow embodied his party or even his country. This concept was built into presidential operations.

The cult of the person, or at least the excesses of it, can be dangerous. It must be kept within reasonable bounds. When issues are so complicated that the people have great difficulty sorting them out, they may decide to trust someone who seems to have some answers - or at least knows the right questions. But the danger is what the Germans proceeded to do when they decided to trust Adolf Hitler. I am not implying that we have reached that point; fortunately, we are still in an area where things can be sorted out and debated.

But the danger is there and must be kept in mind, especially during presidential campaigns. Many people seem to look for a hero, almost a deity, in their candidate. The Greek poet George Seferis wrote a poem that bears on this point. He told of a mule that slipped while carrying the Queen. The Queen fell, broke her neck, and died. Soon after, the spirit of the Queen appeared to the mule-handler and said, "Do not punish the mule. For I was full of the will of God, and that was too much of a burden for any beast to bear."[50]

The Cult of the Expert

Following the elections of 1968, Henry Kissinger, the Nixon assistant in charge of national security, replaced the Johnson assistant, Walt Rostow. The office of assistant for national-security affairs is something new in our government. It is not provided for in the Constitution or in any law passed by the Congress. The powers of the office are undefined, though certainly great.

Mr. Rostow came from the Massachusetts Institute of Technology, Mr. Kissinger from the department of government at Harvard. Mr. Rostow brought with him his best-known book, The Stages of Economic Growth, which hold that a nation goes through more or less certain stages of economic growth. Mr. Kissinger brought as a text his

---

[50] This is a prose version of part of "Three Mules," in George Seferis, Poems, trans. by Rex Warner (London,1960),p.108.

book <u>Nuclear Weapons and Foreign Policy</u>, the thesis of which is that nuclear weapons have brought about a qualitative change in foreign policy. Both Mr. Rostow and Mr. Kissinger are classified as intellectuals.

Borrowing from a remark by G. K. Chesterton, one could say that years ago whenever a problem arose in the United States, someone said that we needed a practical man, and unfortunately there was usually one around.

Acceptance of the intellectual's role in government has been a gradual movement of the past forty years. The role began with the "brain trust" of the Franklin D. Roosevelt administration. Members of that group were never more than consultants who were held at arm's length. The separation of government and the scholars was maintained. President Roosevelt was careful never to arm the clerks with power or even the appearance of power or to admit that they knew more about political problems than did the Cabinet members. His special assistants - men like Harry Hopkins - were identified as practical politicians and special operators.

Although both scholars and intellectuals were present in the Truman and Eisenhower administrations, they were only occasionally noticed, and never cited to sustain political decisions.

In the administration of John Kennedy, there was heavy two-way traffic between the universities particularly Harvard - and the federal government, involving such persons as John Kenneth Galbraith, Arthur Schlesinger, Jr., and McGeorge Bundy. The role of the consultant was acknowledged in most government decisions.

There was no clear evidence that any one of the numerous advisers became the special confidant of President Kennedy or that any one of them had extraordinary influence on his decisions. It remained for President Johnson to give special status to one adviser when he relied so heavily on McGeorge Bundy - and later Walt Rostow - as his special assistant on security matters. This precedent was followed by President Nixon in his appointment and use of Henry Kissinger.

Intellectuals are often thought to be wholly detached and objective on the issues, able to put aside any prejudgment and see problems with greater objectivity and clarity than ordinary mortals. Their opinions are presumed to carry greater weight than the opinions of politicians, sometimes including those of the President. This may or may not be true.

It is interesting that, by the time he was finally appointed Secretary of State, Mr. Kissinger's major achievements had involved the obvious: arranging the long-overdue opening to China and negotiating United States troop withdrawal from Vietnam. Many observers and a fair number of politicians had urged these actions for years, whereas Richard Nixon had opposed them strenuously. But when Kissinger urged such policies, he was viewed as an oracle.

Scholars and intellectuals have an important role as consultants and advisers to government. This is true, first of all, because of the complexity of decisions in science, economics, and general social conditions. It is true, also, because social and cultural change takes place so rapidly today. The lag between the development of theory and its application should be reduced.

On the other hand, the use of the national security assistant contains potential dangers to responsible and representative government. Without challenging the objectivity or intellectual achievements of those who hold the office, one can question the desirability of the office itself.

The first and most serious objection is that the office of security adviser can serve as a shield between the President and the people, thus weakening the lines of responsibility and accountability. It can further insulate the presidency from public scrutiny.

Presidents may eventually claim that their judgments have been influenced by consultation with the pure and unprejudiced minds of their special advisers, in the way medieval kings cited the theologians to justify their policies, and Roman emperors kept soothsayers to read the signs and portents for them.

The successful use of the security adviser could move the President to develop a whole staff of such advisers and to use special advisers for special problems. Thus President Nixon used Sir Robert Thompson, a former English colonial officer and an expert on guerrilla warfare, for advice on Vietnam. There are many former English colonial officers. They may become the vogue in presidential advisers, as were Italian advisers to kings in the late Middle Ages.

The use and the exaltation of special advisers will certainly confuse, if not weaken, the role of the Cabinet and of political parties. It could open the way to general political irresponsibility.

A Good and Becoming Exit

Corporate executives who leave a company or well-known professional athletes who quit a team usually explain their leaving. Clergymen and theologians who leave the church or reject a theological position sometimes explain. But public officials who leave an administration whose position on vital issues they can no longer support usually go quietly. Or they obscure the real reasons with explanations about health, family problems, the need to earn money to educate children, pensions in jeopardy, and so forth. As a result, reasons given for the departures of most officials are so much alike that one scarcely knows whether they have been fired or have resigned.

Samson, a political prisoner, having been blinded by the Philistines, was led out for their sport. The Scriptures say that he "took hold of the two middle pillars upon which the house stood, and on which it was borne up.... And he bowed himself with all his might; and the house fell upon the lords, and upon all the people that were therein."[51] It also fell on Samson. This was a rather violent exit and not one to be recommended as a general practice.

But the effect of a good and becoming exit is not to be discounted. A truly great actor, it is said, is marked by his exits. At best they should be such that, although his going may not have been noticed, his having gone becomes evident.

There are at least eight courses of action open to political officeholders who find themselves dissatisfied with the policies of their government.

-They may continue in service and remain silent.

-They may stay on and try to present their views from within, hoping that they can be more effective than if they left the citadel of power and joined or attempted to lead those outside the walls. The danger here is that one can easily be cast as the devil's advocate, a role George Ball

---

[51] Judges 16:29 30.

accepted in the Johnson administration. Unhappily, the role has serious flaws. The devil's advocate is called on to point out defects in the evidence for beatification or canonization of saints. There is a prejudice against the devil's advocate, since he is cast as one representing the bad side of a good cause.

-They may stay on and murmur against the policy in the gates and porticoes, at dinners and cocktail parties.

-They may stay on and disagree publicly, at least as long as this is allowed. General Douglas MacArthur, when in command of our military effort in Korea, chose to remain in command and also to state his opposition to presidential policy. President Truman responded by dismissing MacArthur. Walter Hickel and Special Watergate Prosecutor Archibald Cox met similar fates in the Nixon administration.

-They may leave quietly and be silent forever. In unusual circumstances silence itself might be construed as protest. Sir Thomas More, who left his position as Chancellor of England when he could no longer support the policy of Henry VIII, was silent for some time. Playwright Robert Bolt has portrayed Thomas Cromwell as complaining, "This 'silence' of his is bellowing up and down Europe!"[52] In the United States the resignation of a Vice President or Secretary of State might have similar impact if followed by silence.

-They may leave quietly, yet in private remarks to columnists or friends make their position public.

-They may leave quietly and be silent until the administration they served is no longer in power, and then state what their views were when they served.

-And finally, they may leave with a frank statement of their reasons for leaving. This is the way least used in American politics.

In the Johnson administration there were several resignations over matters less vital than the war in Vietnam, but none publicly tied to the issue of the war itself. John Gardner, for example, gave up his position as Secretary of Health, Education and Welfare because of differences over national priorities and because the department was not receiving sufficient funds to carry out its programs. Bill Moyers, a presidential aide, went quietly, leaving the impression that he was in

---

[52] A Man for All Seasons, Act II, p. 57.

disagreement with administration policies but not saying anything openly.

Publications and statements issued since the end of the Johnson administration show that many of its members had grave reservations about Johnson's Vietnam policy. Some, such as former Secretary of Defense Robert McNamara, left quietly before the end of the administration and have remained quiet. Others, such as Averell Harriman and former Secretary of Defense Clark Clifford, waited until the end of the administration before stating their views. But no one in a position of real and direct influence on Vietnam policy resigned from the Johnson administration with a statement of opposition to the war. (The same was true of the Nixon people, although Attorney General Elliot Richardson and Deputy Attorney General William Ruckelshaus resigned over the Cox firing. And J. F. terHorst, White House press secretary, resigned early in the Ford administration over the pardon of Mr. Nixon.)

With a touch of scorn, Daniel Berrigan wrote:

One could have wished, when Robert McNamara or Arthur Goldberg stepped off the scene, for some public utterance. Why could such men no longer support the policies of their government? After an iniquitous situation has run its course, another war, another "generation" of weapons, another decade of neglect and destruction, the best the liberals can manage is a tardy, utterly useless statement by some Clark Clifford or other ...[53]

There are some cultural and historical reasons for this. First, there is no tradition of the resignation with purpose in American politics as there is in England and other European democracies.

There are also strong forces in American politics which run against such a dramatic resignation. Loyalty to party and to one's administration is such a force. Governor Nelson Rockefeller received little party support for the Republican presidential nomination in 1968 in part because he had refused to support the party's nominee, Senator Barry Goldwater, in 1964. Most of the candidates

---

[53] Daniel Berrigan, S.J., <u>No Bars to Manhood</u> (New York, 1971), p. 186.

for the Democratic nomination in 1968, even some who opposed the war, were quick to say they would support the party's nominee no matter who he might be or what his platform might be.

There is also the implication, usually encouraged by the administration in power, that anyone who leaves is a quitter, that he is following the recommendation of Harry S. Truman, "if you can't stand the heat you better get out of the kitchen."[54] The answer to this, of course, is that one might well be able to stand the heat but might leave because one does not like what is being cooked up. People who opposed Lyndon Johnson's Vietnam policy were accused of wanting to "cut and run." But the alternative was to be stampeded over the cliff.

In each situation the person involved must consider how to act with integrity and dignity. In some cases the officeholder undoubtedly should stay on; in other cases he should go quietly. But there are also cases in which he should not stay on and should not go quietly or gently.

A man in public office is not wholly free to keep private his views on vital public matters. He must accept the fact that there are times when the public good overrides personal considerations and when loyalty to party or to an office or even to a President must be given a secondary position, a time when, in fact, resignations with explanation are both right and necessary to the public good.

Listen to Mr. Parkinson

Americans have paid little attention to the institutional meaning of public buildings, such as those occupied by Congress. An Englishman, C. Northcote Parkinson, has studied this question with reference to his country. In his book Parkinson's Law, he made significant comments about public buildings and their implications for the vitality of the institutions which use them.

Mr. Parkinson described a building "clothed from the outset with convenience and dignity" and mentioned "the

---

[54] Public Papers of the Presidents: Harry S. Truman, 1952-53 (Washington, 1966), pp. 1085-86, remarks at the Wright Memorial Dinner, December 17, 1952. (Mr. Truman attributed the saying to an "old friend and colleague on the Jackson County Court.")

outer door, in bronze and glass ..." This description could well be applied to the Dirksen Senate Office Building. Parkinson also mentioned the corridors: "Polished shoes glide quietly over shining rubber to the glittering and silent elevator." He noted "the subdued noise of an ordered activity" coming from behind closed doors; he referred to the experience of being "ankle deep" in carpet. All this bears a strong resemblance to conditions in the new Senate and House office buildings.

Mr. Parkinson said that in such a place, "you will feel that you have found real efficiency at last," but that this is not true. "In point of fact you will have discovered nothing of the kind. It is now known that a perfection of planned layout is achieved only by institutions on the point of collapse ..."

Mr. Parkinson's view, one that he illustrated with a history of Parliament buildings in England, was this: "During a period of exciting discovery or progress there is no time to plan the perfect headquarters. The time for that comes later, when all the important work has been done. Perfection, we know, is finality; and finality is death."[55]

In 1960, as a member of the Senate Public Works Committee, I studied Mr. Parkinson's comments on this point and concluded that the recent construction of the second Senate Office Building was a sign of decline of the Senate. There was more room for public-relations people and for service to constituents. In fact, almost every office was becoming a separate political headquarters, not only for those running for the presidency but also for those who were just trying to hold onto their jobs. The Senate was gaining more office space and more employees; yet its effectiveness as a legislature and an influence on the country seemed to decrease almost proportionately.

Madison expected the House to predominate in the government of the country. Applying Parkinson's Law, it can safely be concluded that such is not the case today. The House of Representatives now has three office buildings. The most recent one, the Rayburn, has nine stories, one hundred and sixty-nine congressional suites, twenty-five hearing rooms, a large cafeteria, and an underground garage with capacity for sixteen hundred automobiles. So far this has not made the House of

---

[55] Northcote Parkinson, <u>Parkinson's Law</u> (Boston, 1957), pp. 60-61

Representatives what the men who founded this country intended it to be.

In recent years the Senate tried to reclaim its constitutional role in foreign policy and in other areas. This was cause for some optimism on the part of people who had worried about the decline of the Senate. But in the fall of 1972, the Congress took action which placed institutional renewal of the Senate in doubt. In response to complaints of overcrowding, it authorized a large extension of the Dirksen Senate Office Building and the construction of another parking garage for Senate staff. If precedent is followed, this will result in another increase in the number of Senate employees, more complaints of overcrowding, and eventually a third Senate Office Building.

Perhaps one way for Congress to return to what it was supposed to be in the beginning is to take another look at the building program.

The SST: Object Lesson in Dynamics of Opposition

In March 1971 the Congress voted to end government financing for development of the supersonic transport (SST). Upon hearing of the final vote, one of my daughters said, "Well, at last we have stopped progress."

"Progress" is what supposedly results when American government, business, technology, patriotism, national prestige, and world leadership are mixed in one common effort.

The outstanding recent achievement in the pursuit of progress was the landing of men on the moon. President Nixon said his three greatest thrills were his election to the presidency and two of the moon shots. Some people thought this was a rather expensive way to keep Nixon happy, but opponents of the moon shots were unable to stop them.

Three other projects supported by the military, industry, and organized labor - the TFX, initiation of the ABM system, and the Lockheed loan guarantee - were also challenged, but with little success.

Why did opponents of the SST succeed? Its technological difficulties were no more serious than those associated with the ABM or the TFX. It was not so costly as the moon shots, and its economic potential seemed greater.

A general rule in the Congress is that if there is only one good reason to be against a bad project which has strong support and on which millions have already been spent, the chances of successful opposition are almost nil. If there are two good reasons to be against it, the chances of defeating it are only fair, and the odds remain against a successful challenge. But when there are at least three good reasons for opposition, the project is in real trouble.

By 1971 there were three good reasons for opposing the SST, not all of which were clear when the project was initiated.

The first argument against the SST was the technological one, the chance that its performance would not live up to the projections made for it. Two experiences gave substance to this charge. One was the report of difficulties the British-French combine was having with the Concorde. The other was the loss of confidence in United States aircraft designers because of continuing failures of the TFX (now the F-111) and other planes.

A second major argument against the SST was the economic one, including the cost of producing it and the cost of operating it. The Kennedy administration had put a $750,000,000 limit on public spending for development of the transport. When the appropriation was under consideration in 1971, the estimate was up to $1,300,000,000 and rising, with the possibility that it might go to $4,000,000,000 before production could begin. Because of the indicated high passenger cost per mile, it seemed likely that regular operations would have to be subsidized by the government or covered by higher passenger fares.

The third argument was that of the environmentalists. Proponents of the SST were never able effectively to dispel the fear of noise and air pollution and general dangers to the environment. Warnings of general dangers ranged from increase of the amount of ultraviolet radiation reaching the earth to harmful weather and temperature changes.

For good measure, class discrimination in favor of the rich - especially the jet set - was thrown into the pot. And Senator Charles Percy, one of the last apostles of private enterprise and free trade, argued that the SST should be subjected to the open-market test of private financing.

Incidentally, another element in the defeat of the SST funds was a reform of House rules. A new rule required House members to be recorded by name when voting on amendments in committee of the whole. Previously members had disposed of such amendments by filing down the center aisle to be counted without having their names recorded. The recorded teller vote leaves no place to hide and probably accounted for some of the votes against the SST.

Rejection of the SST marked the achievement of a new level of national maturity. Members of the Congress accepted the fact that the United States need not do everything it can do simply to prove it can do it. They seemed to realize that a first-class power may be distinguished by the things it does not do and does not have to do.

The Lobbyists

The word "lobbying" has a derogatory ring. This is not surprising, for good or bad lobbying occurs at the point of rough transition where interests conflict and judicial processes fall short. Lobbying is a test - sometimes a raw test - of the judgment and integrity of political officeholders, both elected and appointed.

Who are the lobbyists? What do they do in order to affect the course of government? How effective are they? Is lobbying a threat to democracy? What can or should be done about lobbying? It is important that these questions be asked and that an effort be made to answer them.

Lobbying has a long history. The word "lobby" appeared in the English language about the middle of the sixteenth century. It was derived from the medieval Latin word lobium, a monastic walk or cloister. Later the word appeared in politics. It was used both to identify a hall or corridor in the British House of Commons and as a collective noun applied to those who frequented such places. It covered those who sought to influence men in office, as well as newspapermen and others looking for news and gossip.

By statute, the American lobbyist today is a person who is paid for his efforts to influence the passage or defeat of any legislation by the Congress of the United States. But the word "lobbyist" is used both in its narrow

111

legal sense and, more broadly, as a description of one who tries to influence not only the legislators but also any other officers or agencies of government.

No one is sure how many lobbyists - registered and unregistered - there are in Washington, but they probably number in the thousands. The law that requires registration of lobbyists has loopholes and is not really enforced in many cases.

Some lobbyists represent big interests and well-organized groups. The American Petroleum Institute has registered lobbyists along with the American Federation of Labor and Congress of Industrial Organizations (AFL-CIO); so do the Association of American Railroads, the United States Savings and Loan League, and nearly all major industrial and financial interests. And there are lobbyists for many foreign governments.

The "little people" and the less organized also have lobbyists. For example, the American Committee for Flags of Necessity, the Cooperative League of the U.S.A., and the Navajo Tribe are among the groups represented by lobbyists.

The principal "public-interest lobbies" are Ralph Nader's groups and Common Cause. These organizations work for consumer protection, campaign-finance change, congressional reform, and other issues. The environmentalists are represented by groups like Friends of the Earth, which led the successful fight against the SST. Other lobbies carry on the effort for civil rights, peace, and education.

Some lobbyists are well paid; some get little more than expense money. Some operate directly on government officials, others primarily by indirection through appeals to voters. Some are professional, others amateur. Some lobbyists represent only one position or program, while others do freelance work.

Some lobbyists are quite open in seeking their own gain, the protection of an economic advantage, or the elimination of advantages held by competitors. They cry more often for equity than they do for justice. Others speak for the arts, for morality, for aid to the sick and the oppressed among the family of man.

What do lobbyists do in order to affect government decisions?

The methods used by lobbyists are almost as varied as their causes. Some appeal on a purely personal basis, as friend to friend. Some undoubtedly use material appeals. Occasionally there are cases of outright cash bribery; more common, however, are such favors as free rides on company jets or expensive gifts. The indirect influence of campaign contributions is more difficult to assess, but probably more important.

Despite the publicity given to improper influence, the most common method of lobbying is that of simply testifying before a committee of the Congress or speaking to individual members in an attempt to bring them to understand one's position or to influence them to support that position. On issues of particular importance, large organizations like the Chamber of Commerce often organize letter-writing and congressional-visiting campaigns aimed at the entire voting public, using such methods as full-page newspaper ads and speakers' bureaus.

How effective are the lobbyists?

Some are wholly ineffective, yet take credit for what happens without having in any way influenced events. They are known as "rainmakers."

Others, such as the lobbyists of the AFL-CIO, are very effective. The AFL-CIO has won significant victories on such bread-and-butter issues as the minimum wage. It has had a leading role in many successful campaigns for social welfare and civil rights. But it has been unable to achieve one of its major legislative goals: repeal of Section 14(b) of the Taft-Hartley Act. During the Nixon administration it faced occasional congressional defeats, such as the end of government financing for the SST.

The major farm organizations maintain regular lobbies in Washington. The American Farm Bureau Federation and the National Farmers Union often take opposite sides on farm legislation. The apparent success of the two organizations parallels closely the success of the two major political parties. The Farmers Union position is favored when the Democrats are in power, and the Farm Bureau position when the Republicans are in power. In recent years, with control of the government divided between the two parties, it is not surprising that farm programs have, to put it mildly, been confused.

Any significant change in tax laws attracts the attention of those who may be affected. The changes considered in recent years have been significant and controversial, and the lobbying efforts extensive. Special interests have often been able to maintain their tax preferences or to gain new ones.

Industries affected by trade and tariff policies are always well represented in Washington. Whenever an issue even remotely bearing upon trade is brought up for consideration, the representatives of these industries seek permission to testify. Members of the House Ways and Means Committee and the Senate Finance Committee are familiar with the testimony of these witnesses. They have been described as somewhat like professional soldiers who regularly go to battle, seldom win wars, and suffer few casualties.

One of the most active Washington lobbies is that of the American Medical Association - better known in Washington for what it is against than what it is for. The spokesmen for the AMA strongly opposed Medicare when that program was started. More recently, the AMA has opposed legislation to aid health maintenance organizations and legislation to provide comprehensive public health insurance.

The AMA has not been the only group to oppose government involvement in medical care. Some years ago the undertakers testified against one of the government programs on the grounds that it would discourage the traditional doctor-patient relationship. We tried to ease their worries by saying that the program would just provide a slowdown for their profession - that they would still get everyone in the end.

We now come to the basic question: Is lobbying a threat to democracy?

There are some who take the extreme view that lobbies are by their very nature power blocs and therefore inconsistent with democratic government; that since lobbies represent special or limited interests, their objectives are not directed to the general welfare and, therefore, they should be abolished.

There are some who see nothing wrong with lobbies except when they represent economic interests.

There are some who hold that the dangers in lobbying arise from secrecy and behind-the-scenes operations and from the money that may be spent by lobbyists. Thus there are regular demands that more publicity be given to lobbying activities, that lobbying be more closely regulated, and that the amount of money spent by lobbyists be limited and fully reported.

On the positive side, the activity of lobbyists is often helpful. Lobbyists can help maintain a balance between the Congress and the executive branch of the government. The executive branch has a prepared case, usually sustained by expert witnesses. The Congress can offer in opposition the knowledge and experience of its own members and that of committee staff or congressional aides. Often this is an unfair contest. The expert testimony of lobbyists may help to bring the contest closer to balance. (The Congress, of course, does not depend entirely upon lobbyists for its information. It often calls upon independent experts, including ones from the academic profession.)

Apart from laws, there are some built-in protections against the power and influence of lobbyists. One safeguard is that usually there are organized lobbies on both sides of controversial issues: protectionists versus free-traders; the AFL-CIO opposed by the National Association of Manufacturers; antivivisectionists against those who favor medical experimentation with animals; and in recent years, the public-interest lobbies against the special interests.

Political-party positions tend to remove some issues from the influence of lobbyists. The political campaign in the United States is a rather severe testing. Most of the important national issues are raised during political campaigns, and most persons who are elected to office have made commitments on major issues.

Members of the United States Senate must run for re-election every six years, members of the House of Representatives every two years. Their activities are watched closely by colleagues, particularly by those of the opposition party. And they are watched by reporters whose reputations are based on their ability to ferret out and report any conduct unbecoming to government officials. In addition, a man who holds office must assume that there are at least two or three people - perhaps in his own party and certainly in the opposition party - who are quite willing to replace him and therefore are likely to give more than ordinary attention to his conduct in public office.

What can or should be done about lobbying?

Members of Congress cannot be fully protected from lobbyists by regulation. They cannot be expected to keep a check list of registered lobbyists or to demand proof of registration or defense of nonregistration before responding to a request for conversation.

Yet members of Congress and other government officials can be given some protection by law. The present lobby registration act should be clarified and fully enforced, and financial reporting should be checked carefully. Fees contingent on successful lobbying should be outlawed. Care should be taken to remove from direct legislative determination those questions which should be settled by other branches of government: by the President, by the courts, by special commissions, by departments and agencies, or by international agreement. Sounder methods of financing campaigns would reduce improper financial influence on public officials by lobbyists and others.

Lobbying involves organization, a bringing together of citizens seeking a common objective. Thus the act of lobbying is basically an exercise of the right to petition the government - a right set forth in the Constitution. Lobbying also involves, in a way, the right of assembly. It is well to bear in mind these constitutional rights when judging proposals for regulation of the lobbies.

There is always the risk that public officials may be unduly subject to outside influence. But it is hard to imagine a meeting of a national legislature today that could or should be insulated from public pressure or demand. The practice of some primitive tribes, in which the wise men or elders withdrew from society periodically to consider laws and practices, is not likely to be revived.

In a democratic society there must be a point at which influences, both good and bad, are brought to bear upon government. The point at which these influences meet finally is in the elected and appointed officials of the country. These men and women are supposed to be skilled and experienced in politics; they are supposed to have the character to withstand improper pressures and improper demands. Sometimes they do. Sometimes they fail.

Grant Park; Chicago

Morning sun on the pale lake
on plastic helmets, on August
leaves of elm, on grass
on boys and girls in sleeping bags,
curled in question marks.

Asking the answer to the question
of the song and of the guitar
to the question of the fountain,
of the bell and of the red balloon
to the question of the blue kite
of the flowers and of the girl's
brown hair in the wind.

There are no answers
in this park, said the captain
of the guard.

Then give us our questions
say the boys and girls.

The guitar is smashed
the tongue gone from the bell
all kites have fallen, to the ground
or caught in trees
and telephone wires
like St. Andrew, crucified,
hang upside down.
the balloons are broken
flowers faded in the
night fountains have been drained
no hair blows in the wind
no one sings.

Three men in the dawn
with hooks and spears,
three men
in olive drab gathered

all questions into burlap bags.
They are gone --

There are no questions
in this park
said the captain
of the guard.

There are only true facts
in this park
said the captain
of the guard.

Helen did not go to Troy.
The Red Sea never parted.
Leander wore water wings.
Roland did not blow his horn.
Leonidas fled the pass.
Robert McNamara reads Kafka
Kierkegaard and Yeats -- and he said on April 20, 1966,
"The total number of tanks in Latin America is 974,
This is 60 per cent as many as a single country,
Bulgaria, has."[56]

There are only true facts
in this park
said the captain
of the guard.

---

[56] U.S. Senate, Committee on Foreign Relations, *Hearings on Foreign Assistance, 1966*, 89th Congress, session (April 20, 1966), p. 179.

Marching on Washington

Politicians and columnists often busied themselves over the last ten years by analyzing the latest Washington demonstrations, reviewing past demonstrations, making comparisons and evaluations. The general conclusion seemed to be that a few demonstrations were positive, constructive, good, and productive; that others were negative, destructive, bad, and - worst of all - counterproductive. The only objective standard for these distinctions was whether or not there was violence.

There were at least six major Washington marches against the war in Vietnam, each under somewhat different leadership, each with different immediate objectives, each reflecting a different mood.

The first major demonstration took place on October 21, 1967. It was largely spontaneous and unplanned, led or at least spoken for by clergymen and writers. Some fifty thousand persons participated, most of them young and, according to newspaper reports, nearly all of them white. More than one hundred and fifty were seized by police. Among those arrested were a number of adults, including the well-known author Norman Mailer and David Dellinger, chairman of the Mobilization Committee to End the War in Vietnam. The principal target of the march was the Pentagon. Most of the marchers viewed their protest as a symbolic confrontation with the Pentagon. But some small groups tried to rush an entrance there and were repulsed by military police using rifle butts.

Secretary of Defense Robert McNamara spent most of the day at the Pentagon. President Johnson reportedly worked in the White House.

The second major protest took place on November 15, 1969. Estimates of the number of marchers ranged from two hundred and fifty thousand to well over three hundred thousand. Most were young. The line of march was down Pennsylvania Avenue toward the White House. The emphasis of protest was not against the Pentagon, as had been the case in 1967, but against presidential policy. The appeal of the speeches was to reason and to the lessons of history. Tear gas was used against a small group of protesters who moved on the Justice Department.

President Nixon ignored the march. During the massive and generally peaceful protest, he apparently watched a football game on television at the White House. His administration continued to claim the support of a "silent majority" of Americans for its Vietnam policy.

A third march took place on May 9, 1970, shortly after the United States invasion of Cambodia and the killing of four students by National Guardsmen at Kent State University in Ohio. Though organized in haste, this protest drew seventy-five thousand or more people. It was held on the Ellipse, near the White House, and directed against presidential policy. The demonstration was nonviolent, but its rhetoric had a tone of outrage.

President Nixon met with some of the young demonstrators when he stopped by the Lincoln Memorial early on the morning of the demonstration. He sought to defend his policy to them, but evidently with little success.

A fourth major protest was that of April 24, 1971, about one year after the 1970 demonstration and nearly four years after the march on the Pentagon. Estimates of the numbers involved this time ranged from two hundred thousand to three hundred and fifty thousand. Old and young were represented. The line of march this time was not toward the White House, but rather away from it to the foot of the Capitol. The emphasis, as though people had despaired of presidential action and promises, was on what Congress could do to end the war.

Nearly everyone approved of the demonstration. It was well planned, well managed, peaceful, and included as its stars the Vietnam Veterans Against the War, who had stayed on after their own demonstration.

Then there was the 1971 May Day protest, almost a counter-demonstration: not well planned, not well directed, without reputable spokesmen, involving fewer people, without blessing of clergy. It was not directed against the Pentagon as the principal instrument of war or against the White House as source and center of policy. It was not directed to the Congress as a place of residual responsibility. It was directed almost indiscriminately against reality or, just short of that, against those who had little to do with the conduct of the war and even less to do with policy.

There is no way of telling precisely how the antiwar demonstrations affected official opinion or policy. Their principal value seemed to be what they meant, as personal testimony and witness, to those who participated.

In somewhat the same way, many people placed their names on antiwar advertisements in *The New York Times*, making the record but never knowing whether the ads or their names had any effect on policy.

In a sense, the Congress of the protest years did not go much beyond demonstration either. Passing amendments against the war in the Senate was little more than a protest. Senators might just as well have taken a banner and marched around the Capitol for all the effect they were having.

The May Day march of 1971 was the most ineffective by established standards and most open to criticism and ridicule. The numbers taken into custody ran as high as ten thousand persons, many of them teenagers. It gave Vice President Spiro Agnew fodder for another speech or two and encouraged President Nixon to assert that he would not be intimidated by protest.

Despite all the evidence and indications of failure, this protest was in many ways more moving than the earlier, well-programmed and orderly demonstrations. It was the ultimate protest, showing loneliness, frustration, and near despair.

The last major protest against the war was on January 21, 1973 - the day of Richard Nixon's second inauguration. There was the usual debate between police and protest leaders about the numbers marching; police estimated about thirty thousand while protest leaders claimed one hundred thousand.

At the same time that the official inaugural parade proceeded from the Capitol to the White House, the protesters marched from the Lincoln Memorial to the Washington Monument. There was an interesting contrast in the dress of the two groups. The official paraders were in formal dress, whereas the protesters looked like a peasants' army.

Despite expectation of the Vietnam cease-fire that was to be signed the following week, the protesters expressed skepticism about the likelihood of real peace in Southeast Asia. They appeared to be serving notice that they would be back again if the war continued. Their skepticism, it turns out, was well founded.

Changing America

In the course of the past ten years, the young people of this country have been tested as never before in our history. Their moral courage has been tested by the great political issues of our times - the war in Vietnam and racial discrimination at home.

Their physical courage has been tested in many places - in the South all through the 1960s, at the Pentagon in 1967, at Orangeburg, South Carolina, in 1968, at the Chicago convention in the same year, at Kent State University and Jackson State College in 1970, at Southern University in 1972, at countless demonstrations for peace and for civil rights throughout the decade.

They have faced clubs, police dogs, tear gas, mace, and bullets. They have not been found wanting in courage.

Their intellectual commitment, too, has been tested in their efforts to reform the political process, in their analysis of overconsumption and in their opposition to it, and in their support of conservation and environmental programs.

My first political experience with great numbers of young people was in the campaign of New Hampshire in the early months of 1968. They came like the early spring, with a sense of purpose and with promise of change. The older people in that state were glad to see them. Some remarked that they had not talked to their own children in years as they had talked to the young workers of that campaign.

There had been youth and student involvement in other campaigns, in those of Adlai Stevenson and John Kennedy. There were two significant differences, however, between the earlier participation and that of 1968.

The first difference was quantitative. It was estimated that as many as two thousand students campaigned in New Hampshire fulltime during the ten days before the election, and that as many as five thousand joined the effort on weekends. Moreover, they came from all around the country. Students came from New Hampshire colleges and universities and from relatively nearby schools like Harvard, Yale, Smith, and Columbia. But they also came from campuses as far away as Michigan, Wisconsin, Ohio, and even California. Only about half of them were old enough to vote.

The second difference was qualitative and was reflected in the way in which the young participated in the campaign itself. The campaign did not distinguish between an adult and a youth movement. There was a general sharing of responsibility, unrelated to the age of the participant or to his or her experience.

The same pattern of participation marked the later primaries in Indiana, Wisconsin, Oregon, and California. Only the numbers increased.

The cause of the young did not prevail in 1968. They experienced discouragement and failures in politics and in other areas. But their efforts have not been in vain.

They helped turn the nation's attention to the war in Vietnam and to move it to a moral judgment against that war. They participated, and continue to participate, in efforts to lay down a challenge to the militarism of United States foreign policy and to the excessive influence of the military establishment on American life.

They have helped accomplish significant changes in the political process. They were instrumental in insuring voting rights for black people, in achieving party reforms, especially within the Democratic party, and, of course, in getting the vote for persons between the ages of eighteen and twenty-one.

Many persons, young and old, who participated in the 1968 campaign and in other political and social movements have gone onto hold public office. In a recent visit to Wisconsin I was given a folder listing the achievements of some of the persons who had supported me in 1968. In that state the list included the Governor, the State Treasurer, the majority leader of the Wisconsin Assembly, seven members of the state legislature, two city council members, three county board supervisors, and several members of the Democratic National Committee. In the elections of November 1974, Sam Brown, who was one of the most effective youth leaders in my 1968 campaign, was elected State Treasurer of Colorado, and Jerry Brown, who campaigned for me in California in 1968, was elected Governor of that state.

The young people have done much to bring America to a new awareness of the need to preserve our natural resources. Clean air, clean water, and life in harmony with the natural world are again defined and acceptable goals for America.

The young people have challenged excessive consumption, consumerism, and excessive materialism - not just in word and in protest but by the example of their own discipline and simplification of life.

They have also had a significant influence on the institutions closest to them. They have helped free universities from excessive military and corporate influence, often initiating actions that faculty and administrators feared to take. They have achieved desirable procedural and other reforms in many colleges and universities. And young working people have begun to influence labor practices, emphasizing the need to humanize work, to make it satisfying and becoming to human nature.

Not all these things were achieved by youth alone. They were supported in most instances by adults. But in many cases, the leavening force was youth. In many cases, too, the young people bore the greater burden as they carried challenge after challenge into the public field.

PART III Principles

Innocence in Politics

Americans generally are suspicious of politics, and this attitude is far from superficial. It goes much deeper than the public dismay over corruption in government or incompetence in public officials. In fact, the American attitude toward politics shows, more clearly than anything else, a belief in the innocence of Americans. It is a belief that has been a significant force since our colonial era.

As inhabitants of a new land, and living under a new government, Americans from the beginning thought of themselves as also new and innocent, set apart from the stream of tradition and unmarked by history. This attitude continued long beyond our status as a young nation.

Politics is considered by many Americans to be an enemy of innocence and simplicity. Party activity, in particular, is considered degrading by citizens who claim to be nonpartisan. So it is common practice in partisan campaigns to organize citizens' and independents' committees, as distinguished from party committees, to support candidates. These devices are supposed to remove the blight of party identification. Another common device is the use of the term "crusade" to identify one's cause.

The Republican campaign of 1952 provided one of the clearest examples of this technique. General Dwight Eisenhower's supporters insisted that their actions and interests were nonpolitical, that their program was based on moral and spiritual principles. Even in their preliminary conflict with the supporters of Senator Robert Taft, Sr., the Eisenhower forces proclaimed the distinction between the crusaders and the politicians clearly and loudly.

In the 1952 battle over convention delegates, the Taft forces viewed the fight over the Texas delegation as a political one. The Eisenhower supporters would not allow the term "political" to be applied to their side of the battle. They cried that their opponents, as might be expected of politicians, were trying to steal the Texas vote. Similarly they held that the state of Georgia was represented at the convention by good Georgians, supporting their candidate, and by bad Georgians, supporting Senator Taft.

The crusaders' candidate won the Republican nomination. The Taft forces then indicated their willingness to join the crusade, and they were enlisted for the ultimate battle against the real forces of evil - the Democrats. Strange compromises were accepted along the way, as is often the case in crusades after they are launched. A common high purpose was the justification for compromise, as is also usual in crusades.

Twenty years later, a similar drama took place in the Democratic party. This time it was the "McGovern Movement" instead of the "Eisenhower Crusade." McGovern supporters generally regarded themselves as fighting for pure principle; their leader often invoked the Scriptures. The major credentials battles were over the California and Chicago delegations. When the credentials committee decided to take some California votes away from Senator McGovern and award them to other candidates, the Senator called this action "an incredible, cynical, rotten political steal. . . ." But his supporters viewed the successful effort to take delegates away from Mayor Richard Daley as an exercise of justice and a victory for principle.

The assumption of innocence in politics has serious weaknesses when tested by adversity, whether in a campaign or in a new administration. For the innocent naturally inclines to false optimism and oversimplification. When beset by difficulty, his first inclination is to delay and postpone, to shun hard choices, to hope for change.

Complexity or setback, even of a temporary nature, is difficult for the innocent to explain or to bear. For he assumes that his intentions are good and his cause is just and that, consequently, immediate and continuous success should be assured. When success does not follow and delay is no longer possible, the innocent tends to choose the compromise position and to view this choice as the ideal. The innocent may also postpone admission of failure by raising a hue and cry against wicked men who may be about to seek a scapegoat, a person to be blamed, a Jonah to be cast into the sea.

Statements of innocence and simplicity can solve few problems in a world that is complex and beyond innocence. In the words of Sir Thomas More, "For it is not possible for all things to be well, unless all men are good - which I think will not be this good many years."[57]

Language and Politics

Man has never fully escaped the Tower of Babel nor avoided the confusion of tongues. Man lives by words, and the use of words is, therefore, always a serious and a dangerous act. Patrick Henry's "give me liberty, or give me death"[58] was an inspiration for and a significant part of the American Revolution. With the words J'accuse, Emile Zola[59] stirred the French nation against the injustice of the Dreyfus case. And Churchill in the early months of World War II gave courage and resolution to England: "We shall fight on the beaches ..."[60]

Poets and men of letters are the special custodians of language. Scientists and mathematicians seek stabilization of meaning through the use of symbols rather than words: $E = mc^2$ was Einstein's word.

The Catholic Church long used Latin as the language of official doctrine and ritual, claiming it is universal, immutable, and independent of the weaknesses of vernacular languages. But the fact is, as theologians know, even a dead language does not help. People are perverse. They think and believe and die in the language they live in.

In a democracy the language of politics is of special concern. The theoretical basis of a democracy supposes a measure of good will in people, so that when they are informed, they can make sound political judgments. For this theory to work, there must be a common language. If the language is debased or misused, if the meaning of

---

[57] Thomas More, The Utopia of Sir Thomas More, ed. by Mildred Campbell (New York, 1947), p. 61.

[58] Patrick Henry, quoted in William Wirt, Sketches of the Life and Character of Patrick Henry (Philadelphia, 1817), p. 123, speech of March 23, 1775.

[59] J'accuse: Émile Zola, La Vérité en Marche (Paris, 1901), pp. 91 open letter of January 13, 1898, to Félix Faure, President of the Republic.

[60] Winston S. Churchill, Blood, Sweat, and Tears (New York, 1941), p. 297, speech in the House Commons, June 4, 1940.

words is obscure, the basis for common judgment is undermined, if not destroyed.

The pressure on the language of politics is always greatest when political problems are most difficult and when politicians are called upon to answer for failure in other professions.

The war in Vietnam subjected the language of American politics to severe strain. That strain was reflected in three general ways: first, in the growing use of words derived from Latin; second, in the use of old words with new meaning; and third, in the development of new words.

George Orwell, in an essay written in 1946, said that when political writers and speakers are called on to defend the indefensible, they turn to Latin. Then, according to Orwell, "A mass of Latin words falls upon the facts like soft snow, blurring the outlines and covering up all the details."[61]

"Escalation" was the principal Latin derivative used in talking about the Vietnam war. It may not fall on the facts like snow, but it is a useful word, for it does not permit fixing a point of decision. It has no beginning, no intermediate point, no ending. It is an uncaused, continuing condition without a before or an after.

The word "pacification," basically a Latin word, in its Orwellian redefinition encompasses bombing villages, driving inhabitants into the countryside, machine-gunning cattle, and burning huts.

"Incursion," another word of Latin derivation, was used by the Nixon administration to describe its activity in Cambodia in the spring of 1970. The choice of the word was curious, for there is no verb form for "incursion." An army cannot simply "incurse," though it can invade. Incursions simply take place, without before or after. An incursion is absolute, existential, out of any context of time or judgment.

As serious in their consequences as the Latinization of the vocabulary were the new definitions. One needed a special dictionary to understand reports on the progress of this war. "Selective ordnance" was napalm. "Resources control" had reference to chemical poisoning of crops. "Tactical evacuees" were refugees from villages that were

---

[61] George Orwell, "Politics and English Language," in A Collection of Essays (New York, 1954), p. 173.

to be destroyed for military purposes. "Benevolent incapacitators" sounded like items that might be helpful to people, like painkillers or sleeping pills. But the term referred to types of gas that, although not killers in themselves, often caused vomiting and other physical distress and were sometimes lethal in their indirect effects.

New words were also employed. President Nixon, in a speech of November 3, 1969, stressed the word "Vietnamization." The closely related word of "Vietnamizing" had been explained the previous month in a speech by Secretary of Defense Melvin Laird.

The Johnson administration, according to Mr. Laird, had a policy of partially de-Americanizing the war. The Nixon administration, he said, had a policy of "Vietnamizing" the war. There was, he added, an enormous difference between these two policies."[62] Perhaps there was, but that difference was not evident in action nor was it clearly indicated in the Secretary's distinctions.

A new term that was particularly imaginative was "reinforced protective reaction flights." Senator Fulbright was not awed by the new vocabulary; he said, "We call them bombing raids in the Ozarks."[63] "Destabilization" was the CIA word for aiding the 1973 overthrow of the Chilean government.

The real danger in use of the new language is not so much that the public is deceived - although there is danger of that - but that those who make the decisions begin to think and issue orders in neutral or amoral language, in language they would not normally use to make intellectual or moral judgments.

Some Green Berets apparently were ordered to "terminate with extreme prejudice"[64] as they prepared to act against a Vietnamese agent. No English-speaking person under ordinary circumstances would have interpreted this as an order to execute the agent. The Green Berets evidently did. It is easier to order the termination of a relationship than to order an execution,

---

[62] Melvin Laird, quoted in the *Washington Star*, October 7, 1969, p. A 3.

[63] J. William Fulbrigbt, quoted Mary McGrory, "New Rhetoric With LBJ's Brand," *Washington Star*, May 5, 1970, p. A 17.

[64] *The New York Times*, August 14, 1969, p. 2.

easier to report that a relationship has been terminated than to report that a man has been killed.

The original *New York Times* report of the events at the My Lai 4 hamlet, Song My village, on March 16, 1968, said:

> *American troops caught a North Vietnamese force in a pincer movement on the central coastal plain yesterday, killing 128 enemy soldiers in daylong fighting....*
>
> *While the two companies of United States soldiers moved in on the enemy force from opposite sides, heavy artillery barrages and armed helicopters were called in to pound the North Vietnamese soldiers.*
>
> *The American command's military communiqué said fighting continued sporadically through the day. The action ended at 3 p.m., when the remaining North Vietnamese slipped out and fled, according to the communiqué...*[65]

We now know that something quite different happened there. And it was not something that happened out of context. In August 1967, according to Jonathan and Orville Schell, who reported on this period of the war, during Operation Benton, the "pacification" camps became so full that Army units in the field were ordered not to "generate" any more refugees. The Army complied. But search-and-destroy operations continued. Only now peasants were not warned before an air strike was called in on their village. They were killed in their villages because there was no room for them in the swamped pacification camps....[66]

By March 1968 the language of the orders had shifted from the negative of not to "generate any more refugees" to the positive of destroying the My Lai 4 hamlet, and then the specific and final word of officer to soldier, "I want them dead."[67]

---

[65] *The New York Times*, March 17, 1968, pp. 1 and 5.

[66] Jonathan and Orville Schell, *The New York Times*, November 26, 1969, p. 44, letter to the editor.

[67] Lieutenant William L. Calley, Jr., quoted Seymour H. Hersh, My Lai 4 (New York, 1970), p. 50.

The original, high-level discussions and decisions evidently were all made without the use of the basic and ultimate words, "kill" and "dead" - without recognition, that is, of the realities facing a soldier under orders in the village of Song My.

While some military terms were softened for use in Vietnam, others were used in their original sense to describe our domestic programs. Thus we had a war on poverty, followed at various times by a war on ignorance, a war on hunger, a war on cancer, a war on drug abuse. Efforts to end such afflictions might proceed more intelligently if separated from the military psychology.

The same might be said of other programs. The term "health care delivery system" bears an interesting resemblance to "missile delivery system." And it is not particularly helpful to speak of a communications system that is aimed at a "target population."

Our country will be well served if we can restore to its politics a decent respect for language and for life.

Poetry and War

On being asked for a war poem, William Butler Yeats responded with these lines:

> *I think it better that in times like*
> *these*
> *A poet's mouth be silent, for in truth*
> *We have no gift to set a statesman*
> *right;*
> *He has had enough of meddling who*
> *can please*
> *A young girl in the indolence of her*
> *youth,*
> *Or an old man upon a winter's night.*[68]

And André Gide observed during World War II, "The war warps all minds....In short, everything urges me to frank silence."[69]

Despite the admonitions of men like Yeats and Gide, modern writers, especially poets, have written about war and in wartime, as their poet predecessors had written about war since the beginning of written language. Before them, the minstrels and rhymers had a go at war and battles with whatever spoken language they had available.

The results have not been very good.

According to Sir Thomas Herbert Warren, a British poetry professor during World War I, the task is difficult if not impossible: "War, when it is really exhausting, crushes out, or burns up, poetry. It enfeebles the body politic, absorbs the interest, and lowers the vitality of a nation...."[70]

The best war poetry is descriptive, and as such not very different from prose.

---

[68] W. B. Yeats, "On Being Asked for a War Poem," in The Collected Poems of W. B. Yeats (New York, 1956), 153.

[69] André Gide, The Journals of André Gide, trans. by Justin O'Brien (New York, 1951), Vol. IV, p. 6.

[70] Thomas Herbert Warren, Poetry and War (London [1915]), p. 8.

There is an inherent difficulty in writing poetry of war, which is that the reality defies imaginative or creative interpretation. War does not lend itself to metaphor, which might make it more understandable or give it meaning.

To what does one compare the realities described in the following lines from "The Long War" by the Chinese poet Li Po?

> *The gray ravens and hungry vultures tear,*
> *And carry away the long bowels of the dead,*
> *Hanging them on the twigs of lifeless trees.*[71]

Or these from the poem "'They'" by Siegfried Sassoon?[72]

> *"We're none of us the same!" the boys reply.*
> *"For George lost both his legs; and Bill's stone blind;*
> *Poor Jim's shot through the lungs and like to die;*
> *And Bert's gone syphilitic; you'll not find*
> *A chap who's served that hasn't found some change."*

Or these images from "The Unknown Soldier" by Walter Benton?[73]

And I was dredged out of the Rapido or the Rhine,
the Neckar, the Moselle,
recovered from debris of Anzio or Aachen...Bastogne, St. Lo-
face leveled, dogtags blown off.

Charred past recognition in a gas-drenched tank....

A body in the image of God was lying on the plain,
the maggot and the bluebottle cast dice for it
and black bald birds swung lower and lower for their cut....

Except for the rhyme and the counted syllables, all these might well pass for prose, for there is scarcely a poetic image in the lot - only simple, stark description.

---

[71] Li Po, "The Long War," trans. by Cheng Yu Sun, in Richard Eberhart and Selden Rodman, ed., War and the Poet (New York, 1945), p. 44.

[72] Siegfried Sassoon, "'They,'" in Robert Cromie, ed., Where Steel Winds Blow (New York, 1968), p. 119.

[73] Walter Benton, "The Unknown Soldier," in Cromie, p. 106.

Since metaphor is the essential method of poetry, to attempt poetry where metaphor is practically unusable is to attempt the near impossible. Moreover, the way of good poetry is that of downward comparison. The poor poet may compare persons to angels or to God, a pointless effort since we know less of angels and of God than we do of man. To compare man to animals is something different. Since we have some understanding of various animals, the comparison may tell us something about the person described. Seldom, if ever, do we find a pig described as manlike, but we do find in poetry and in common language pigs or other animals used for comparison in order to make more clear the character of a person. The proper study of man, for the poet, is not man or God as much as it is animals and other lesser but better understood realities.

Unable to deal with their subject matter in the ways of poetry and to give deeper meaning or fuller understanding to war, many poets take the easy way out and write of it as without meaning. Thus Byron[74] wrote in "Don Juan":

> *A moderate pension shakes full many a sage,*
> *And heroes are but made for bards to sing,*
> *Which is still better; thus in verse to wage*
> *Your wars eternally, besides enjoying*
> *Half-pay for life, makes mankind worth destroying.*

And Richard Le Gallienne[75] in "The Illusion of War":

> *Art, thou hast many infamies,*
> *But not an infamy like this.*
> *Oh, snap the fife and still the drum,*
> *And show the monster as she is.*

And Carl Sandburg[76] in "Grass":

> *Pile the bodies high at Austerlitz and Waterloo.*
> *Shovel them under and let me work --*
> *I am the grass; I cover all.*

---

[74] George Gordon, Lord Byron, Don Juan, canto 8, stanza 14.

[75] Richard Le Gallienne, "The Illusion of War," in Vincent Godfrey Burns, ed., The Red Harvest (New York, 1930), p. 3.

[76] Carl Sandburg, "Grass," in Eberhart and Rodman, p. 136.

All of which, insofar as understanding is concerned, leave us just about where we came in.

Some poets blame war on God, directly or indirectly, and ask God to explain. The tradition has a long history. For Virgil[77] it was "the savagery of bloody Mars." Siegfried Sassoon[78] ended one of his war poems with this line:

> And the Bishop said: "The ways of God are strange!"

And Robert Lowell[79] wrote in his poem "The Bomber":

> Did you know the name of flight
> When you blasted the bloody sweat
> And made the noonday night:
> When God and Satan met
> *And Christ gave up the Ghost?*

Generals, politicians, and old men come in for their share of blame. Li Po[80] wrote:

> *0 soldiers who fight long --*
> *Their blood varnishes the desert weeds!*
> *But the generals who lead them on --*
> *They have accomplished nothing!*

And William Cowper[81]:

> *Great princes have great playthings....*
> *Some seek diversion in the tented field*
> *And make the sorrows of mankind their sport.*

And Witter Bynner[82], in his poem "The Old Men and the Young Men":

---

[77] Virgil, the *Georgics*, in Eberhart and Rodman, p. 32.

[78] Sassoon, "'They,'" in Cromie, p. 119.

[79] Robert Lowell, "The Bomber," in Eberhart and Rodman, p. 209.

[80] Li Po, "The Long War," in Eberhart and Rodman, p. 44.

[81] William Cowper, "Playthings," in Eberhart and Rodman, pp. 78 79.

[82] Witter Bynner, "The Old Men and the Young Men," in Cromie, p. 162.

Said the old men to the young men,
"Who will take arms to be free?"
Said the young men to be free"
"We."

Walter Benton[83] ended "The Unknown Soldier" this way:

And in the last world, quarrelsome old men
convened in domed halls and bannered parliaments to vote
for a vast, splendid, residential tomb.

Theology, psychology, or historical criticism takes over nearly every one of these poetic efforts. The poetry is smothered.

The wars in which the United States has been involved have not produced poetry of any significant note. America was not very poetic at the time of the Revolution. That was a war of nonfiction; the inspiration came from the pens of men who were masters of prose. But since soldiers do sing (and then did march) in rhythm, old songs and rhythms were adapted for the war. "Yankee Doodle" is the best known survivor.

The Civil War is best remembered for its prose and for its songs. Julia Ward Howe's "Battle Hymn of the Republic" helped set the moral tone for the Union cause, as General Albert Pike's version of "Dixie" did for the South. There were other songs: "John Brown's Body," "Maryland, My Maryland" by James Ryder Randall, "Tenting on the Old Camp Ground" by Walter Kittredge, "Marching through Georgia" by Henry Clay Work, and many more.

The straight poetry of the Civil War was largely partisan and openly inspirational. Henry Timrod wrote of Charleston, Paul Hamilton Hayne of Vicksburg, Abram Joseph Ryan of "The Conquered Banner" for the South. John Greenleaf Whittier[84], for the North, gave us the poem "Barbara Frietchie" with the memorable or at least much memorized lines:

"Shoot, if you must, this old gray head,
But spare your country's flag," she said.

---

[83] Walter Benton, "The Unknown Soldier," in Cromie, p. 107.

[84] John Greenleaf Whittier, "Barbara Frietchie," in The Patriotic Anthology (New York, 1941), p. 205.

Walt Whitman[85], who cared for the wounded and sick of both Northern and Southern armies, did not take sides or attempt to explain the war in his poetry. The closest he came to such writing was in "I Saw the Vision of Armies," with its conclusion that the dead were the only ones

... fully at rest - they suffer'd not;
The living remain'd and suffer'd - the mother suffer'd,
And the wife and the child, and the musing comrade suffer'd,
And the armies that remained suffer'd.

One would not list these lines among the best of Whitman.

Sir Thomas Herbert Warren said that some wars are "best commemorated, not by contemporaries, but by poets of a later time writing when peace and her arts had plucked up heart and merriment again."[86]

Whereas one hesitates to say that Allen Tate and Robert Lowell writing long after the Civil War, were writing when "peace and the arts had plucked up heart and merriment again," Tate's "Ode to Confederate Dead" and Lowell's "For the Union Dead" are perhaps the best poems written about the Civil War. They sustain Warren's judgment.

World War I produced mixed poetry. The best of it, like that of Siegfried Sassoon and Wilfred Owen, was highly personal, morbid and sometimes detached from the war. The songs of that war, in contrast with the poetry, were generally carefree and irreverent. It may have been, as a recent governor of Indiana observed, the "only war that was a happy one."[87]

World War II produced poetry and songs different from those of World War I. Hitler and Axis Sally were different from Kaiser Bill and Mademoiselle from Armentières. The invasion army was different from the American Expeditionary Force. The helmets were German and pragmatic -- different from the rakish, plate-like helmets of World War I. World War II songs were of home, of

---

[85] Walt Whitman, "I Saw the Vision of Armies," in Eberhart and Rodman, p. 105.

[86] *Poetry and War*, p. 9.

[87] Roger Branigan, quoted in Lewis Chester et al., *An American Melodrama* (New York, 1969), p. 169.

White Cliffs Of Dover, of White Christmases. The poetry was less personal than that of World War I, as the war too was less personal. It was good when the war was almost incidental to its writing, as was the case with Karl Shapiro's wartime poems, and not very good when written about the war itself, as were Robert Lowell's poem "The Bomber" and Randall Jarrell's "Eighth Air Force." World War II belonged to the novelists: James Jones, Norman Mailer, James Michener, James Gould Cozzens, and others.

This leaves only the war in Vietnam and the poetry it provoked or elicited. ("Inspired" would scarcely be the right word.)

If most wars are beyond poetic treatment, certainly one would think this of the Vietnamese war. It was beyond poetry, but it was also beyond prose and somehow came back to the poets. They did not refuse.

It was a war that was not only "not happy," if I may again refer to the former governor of Indiana, but positively unhappy for most Americans and for nearly all poets. Some poets took it on with enthusiasm, but others reluctantly, in the mood of the Irish poet Austin Clarke, who said, "I have written a poem about the war - not a very good one. It is hard to write good poetry about that war, but one must try."[88]

With no exception that I know of, American poets who have written of the Vietnam war, established or not, professional or not, recognized or not, published or not, have been bitterly critical of the war and of those whom they hold responsible for it.

The titles of some of the poems indicate the themes and thrust:

"The Grate Society" by George Bowering

"Thinking of Vietnam after Reading The Iliad" by Richard Snyder

"A Hellenic Sonnet for Mr. Johnson on His Refusal of Peter Hurd's Official Portrait" by Richard Wilbur

"Burning the News" by Lewis Turco

"Counting Small-Boned Bodies" by Robert Bly.

So does the volume of poetry entitled Winning Hearts and Minds. This consists of poetry by Vietnam veterans,

---

[88] Austin Clarke, in a conversation with the writer, Dublin, Ireland, March 1970.

nearly all bitter, apologetic, angry, distressed, near despair -- not much good poetry, but a total statement on the war, a laying bare of self by way of purgation. Why else would Larry Rottmann write and publish the following?[89]

> *Ask what kind of war it is*
> *where you can be pinned down*
> *all day in a muddy rice paddy*
> *while your buddies are being shot*
> *and a close-support Phantom jet*
> *who has been napalming the enemy*
> *wraps itself around a tree and explodes*
> *and you cheer inside*

It is a partial response to what is said and asked in the poem "That Painter in the City" by the Vietnamese poet Tu Ke Tuong[90]:

I

In the morning you just wake up when that painter suddenly
splashes a swarm of green leaves
everyone of us we see the sun suspended in air
but not that painter
he insists on thinking it a ripe fruit
and so he paints on the citreous background
a strange perfume.

II

when he turns mad and jumps on the sandbag to perform
the children crowd round and cheer
the painter draws a ripe grenade hanging from a branch
and he loudly proclaims to the multitude
everlasting peace
he also points out to everyone
a sunbaked corpse loitering on the fence
then he adds to it just a touch of remaining fresh blood.

III

and when the blind bird is with child
he sketches on our eyes a pair of wooden crutches
and says here is enduring happiness
to illumine your blackened days

IV

---

[89] Larry Rottmann, "What Kind of War?" in Rottmann et al., ed., *Winning Hearts and Minds* (New York, 1972), p. 97.

[90] Tu Ke Tuong, "That Painter in the City," from <u>A Thousand Years of Vietnamese Poetry</u>, ed. Nguyen Ngoc Bich (New York, 1975).

then the day we lie down
that painter again strokes a fresh green meadow
he says that's a cool and comfortable bed
and every morning
he adds innumerable fragrant blossoms
as we start to forget to breathe little by little.

Sometimes poets are the last resort. And as Austin Clarke said, although it was hard to write good poetry about the war in Vietnam, they did try.

Ares

god, Ares
is not dead.
he lives,
where blood and water mix
in tropic rains.
no, NNE, or S
or W, no compass --
only mad roosters
tail down on twisted vanes
point to the wind
of the falling sky
the helicopter wind
that blows straight down
flattening the elephant grass
to show small bodies crawling
at the roots, or dead
and larger ones
in the edged shade, to be counted
for the Pentagon, and
for The New York Times.

ideologies can make a war
last long and go far
ideologies do not have boundaries
cannot be shown on maps
before and after
or even on a globe
as meridian, parallel
or papal line of demarcation.

what is the line between
Moslem and Jew
Christian and Infidel
Catholic and Huguenot
with St. Bartholomew waiting
on the calendar for his day
to come and go?
what map can choose between cropped heads
and hairy ones?

what globe affirm
"better dead than red"
"better red than dead"?
ideologies do not bleed
they only blood the world.

mathematical wars go farther.
they run on ratios
of kill and overkill
from one to x
and to infinity.
we are bigger, one to two
we are better, one to three
death is the measure
it's one of us to four
of them, or eight to two
depending on your point of view.
12 to 3
means victory
12 to 5 forebodes defeat.
these ratios stand
sustained
by haruspex and IBM.
we can kill all of you
three times
and you kill all of us
but once and a half -- the game
is prisoner's base, and we
are fresh on you
with new technology.

we sleep well
but worry some. We know
that you would kill us twice
if you could, and not leave
that second death half done.
we are unsure
that even three times killed
you might not spring up whole.
snakes close again
and cats do, it is true
have nine lives. Why
not the same for you?
no one knows about third comings
we all wait for the second, which

may be bypassed
in the new arithmetic.
or which, when it comes
may look like a first
and be denied.

the best war, if war must be
is one for Helen
or for Aquitaine.
no computation stands
and all the programmed lights
flash
and burn slowly down to dark
when one man says
I will die
not twice, or three times over
but my one first life, and last
lay down for this my space
my place, my love.

Intellectuals and Politics

A superficial reading of the political history of the United States supports the view that American politics is anti-intellectual and that, American government is a product of the efforts of "practical" men.

Certainly the founding fathers were practical men. In writing and then defending the Declaration of Independence, they took practical political action - knowing that the consequence of failure was almost certain execution as traitors.

American politics is idealistic at the same time, and the reported division between politics and idealism is more fancied than real.

The failure to associate politics with the philosophical and intellectual arena of ideas has sometimes arisen from the very absence of genuine ideological conflict between men of ideas and men of action in American political life. Certainly philosophers, historians, and men of ideas were accepted as associates and advisers of politicians in the earliest days of our history.

G. K. Chesterton[91], in his book What I Saw in America, published in 1922, said that

America is the only nation in the world that is founded on a creed. That creed is set forth with dogmatic and even theological lucidity in the Declaration of Independence; perhaps the only piece of practical politics that is also theoretical politics and also great literature.

The creed to which he referred was expressed in the Declaration in these words:

We hold these Truths to be self-evident, that all Men are created equal, that they are endowed by their Creator with certain unalienable Rights, that among these are Life, Liberty, and the Pursuit of Happiness....

These words and these ideas were taken seriously by the men who drafted the Declaration of Independence.

---

[91] G. K. Chesterton, What I Saw in America (London, 1922), p. 7.

They were written by men in danger of being shot or hanged if the Revolution they led turned out to be a failure. The words and the ideas they expressed were taken literally. They were not stated merely as a justification for the Revolution, but were intended to establish a foundation in principle upon which democratic institutions and traditions could be established anywhere in the world. What was incorporated in the early documents was a product of the whole tradition of Western political thought from Plato to the humanist and rationalist philosophers of the eighteenth century.

The fields of study and of intellectual pursuit which bear most directly upon politics today are these three: history, economics, and moral or ethical science.

Politicians throughout history have been somewhat concerned about their place in history and about the movement of history as it has affected their own countries and their own political action. Great military and political leaders of the past sometimes appointed their own historians or even served as historians of their own achievements. They often ordered the construction of their own arches and temples. They patronized artists and poets who in turn were expected to do well by them in the artistic record.

In the nineteenth and early twentieth centuries, the disposition to set one's own country apart from history, to assert its independence and unique character, was very common among Western nations. What passed for history or for political philosophy in too many cases was self-justifying and fictional.

Extremes of nationalism are always something of a threat to historians and to history, since leaders of a strongly nationalistic state, or those who speak for it, are inclined to believe that it is somewhat above or outside history. They tend to think of themselves as the center and focal point of history, to minimize the efforts of the past, and to assume that the patterns they establish will be the model for the indefinite future. The questions of continuity and of relations to the movement of history itself are discounted.

Nearly every politician today who says with some certainty that Columbus discovered America in 1492 is said to have a sense of history. Viewed in a broader context, such observations reflect concern for an understanding of history and a hope that those responsible for government will interpret their own times and will make political decisions within the context and the movement of history.

In the period since the end of World War II, we have come to recognize that the mass of current history and the speed of history make special demands both upon governments and upon people. The mass or the volume of those things which demand our attention is greater than it has ever been. Political responsibility today extends to the whole world. We can no longer set aside whole continents or whole nations or whole races as though they were not a part of contemporary history. We have to accept, and in some measure we must give attention to, all peoples in all places. There is no place in the world today and no person in the world for which we do not have some degree of obligation and responsibility.

But along with the increase in volume, there is a second most significant consideration: the speed of the change and development today is at a rate which is faster than it has ever been before. We are not called on to respond to a timetable or a schedule of our own making - much as we would like to have it that way; rather, we are called upon to respond on the basis of a schedule which the movement of history imposes upon us.

The second intellectual discipline bearing upon politics in a direct way is economics. I do not mean to exclude other social sciences as having no bearing upon government and government decisions, nor would I discount the influence of the natural sciences on our culture. But in a very special and direct way, economic theory has come to play a great role in government economic and fiscal policy.

Some attention was given to economics by government in the period of the Great Depression in the United States. Theories of business cycles were developed. What in rather popular political terms was described merely as Keynesian economics became the limited guide for political economy.

In 1962 President Kennedy requested discretionary power to reduce personal income tax rates within limits and thereby stimulate the economy by increasing citizens' take-home pay. In 1963 President Kennedy urged the Congress to cut taxes in order to stimulate economic growth and expansion. This was a new kind of argument for a tax cut. It challenged several accepted ideas in the field of political economy: first, and the principal one, that in times of prosperity budgets should be balanced and federal deficits reduced; second, that federal deficits inevitably resulted in inflation; and third, that government expenditures by their very nature were wasteful and noneconomic.

For anyone prepared to challenge those three points, it was almost as important to make a moral case as it was to make an economic one. Economists and others, therefore, had to make it clear that they were not in any absolute or moral sense in favor of unbalanced budgets; that they were not in any absolute or moral sense in favor of inflation - either galloping or creeping; that they did not believe that governmental spending was never wasteful. Each of these propositions, it was argued, had to be judged in the total context of the needs of the country and, therefore, related to questions of war and peace and to the condition of the economy, both domestic and international.

Today, when our economic problems are more serious than in 1963, the importance of economics is obvious. Perhaps less obvious is the need for new interpretations, new theory. We are beyond Keynes. An economist or politician who refused to accept this would be somewhat like a physicist who insisted that only the theories of Newton could be applied.

The third intellectual discipline relevant to politics today is moral or ethical science.

The influence of moralists is most often indirect. Ethics defines the ends and purposes of political power and judges the methods and conditions of the use of political power. But the combination and application is the work of politics.

Moralists, Jacques Maritain said, are unhappy people; so are politicians. Maritain believed that the task of ethics is a humble one. The task of the politician is, in a sense, even more humble than that of the moralist. It is also rather difficult. The fundamental objective of politics is to bring about progressive change in keeping with the demands of social justice. Politics is concerned with ways and means and with prudential judgments as to what should be done, when it should be done, and in what measure and how it should be done. The politician should be a moralist himself; in any case, he must pay attention to the voice of the moralist.

The concern of moralists with the great questions of war and peace has had significant consequences in the last decade. Historians said of the war in Vietnam that it was not justified by history, and economists manifested concern over the effects the war was having on our economy. But the most telling argument was left to moralists and philosophers, who concluded that methods used in the war were morally indefensible and that the violence employed was out of all proportion to any goal that might be won. Their judgment had influence on politicians and also on those who had been called upon to fight the war.

Intellectuals today must deal with serious contradictions. On one hand, in the second half of the twentieth century, people have more freedom than ever before. They are more truly and completely human because they are more free from nature, more free from ignorance, more free from the material limitations of the past, more free of the past itself. On the other hand, there has been a growing separation between reason and life, means and end, society and the individual, religion and morality, action and sensibility, language and thought, men in the community and men in the crowd.

In recent centuries, many intellectual leaders were not as directly and immediately involved in the life and problems of their times as they should have been. They were guilty of indifference, detachment, and withdrawal. The gods could climb higher on Olympus and thus avoid the clamor of the world and of the crowd.

In the eighteenth and nineteenth centuries there was a growing rejection of theology and philosophy, and even of history. There was an arrogant assertion that science and technology and new political and economic forms would provide the answers which philosophy and theology and other intellectual disciplines had failed to provide in the past.

The excuse of rejection no longer stands. The world today is not arrogant. It has been brought low. The world today does not suffer from illusion.

There is, of course, still a need for the long view and the search for absolutes, but there is also a great need for the application of that knowledge which we do possess to contemporary life and problems. The dead hand of the past is less of a problem - although we still use it as an excuse - than is the violent hand of the future, which reaches back for us today, imposing most serious demands.

There is little time to escape, and few escape routes are still open. Some may wish to take the advice of Bob Hope, given in a commencement address some years ago, when in mock humor he advised the graduates not to go out and face the world. Or a similar escape suggested by my son when he was very young: when asked what he would have liked to be had he lived in ancient Roman times an emperor, a soldier, or a martyr - he said that he would have preferred to be a lion.

Full withdrawal or retreat is no longer possible. Intellectual spokesmen and moral leaders are called upon today to prove the relevance of their ideas to life. By necessity of history rather than by choice, those who have long been pilgrims of the absolute are forced now to become pilgrims of the relative as well.

Intellectual and moral leaders today cannot retreat in ignorance and half-truths or go back into their own protected caves. Leonardo da Vinci could speculate on the principles of aerodynamics without giving any thought to the possibility that his knowledge would be used to construct intercontinental ballistic missiles. Rene Descartes could develop new theories of mathematics without anticipating that his conclusions might be incorporated in nuclear bombs. Intellectuals of the past did not have to anticipate what might happen to their ideas when subjected to the power of computers.

Time has caught up with the intellectuals. Their advance positions have been overrun.

The alternative to reasoned direction of life is a return to primitive conditions of ignorance and false fear. If we believe that man is the subject of history rather than simply the object (an object controlled by economics or by some irrational force), if we acknowledge that the period of half-civilization and half-knowledge of the nineteenth century has been shattered, if we accept that we must face the judgment of our nation and of our age, then we need a full and reasoned response from the intellectuals.

We must reaffirm our confidence in reason as the one truly human instrument that we must use for guidance and direction as we continue to live on the edge of disaster. Both the intellectual and the politician must continue to pass reasoned judgment on life and history, for without knowing, there can be no proper doing.

Out of Phase

No society can make orderly progress unless its philosophy, its policies, and its programs are reasonably in phase. Philosophy, policy, and program were in phase at the founding of our country. Thomas Jefferson, John Adams, and their fellow conspirators had a philosophy of government and of social organization. They had policies by which they sought to make that philosophy a reality in history. They had a program: the Revolutionary War and the establishment of a new government. It all went together.

Today, in almost every major area of political and social concern, philosophy, policy, and program are out of phase. We have in some areas more philosophy than we have either policy or program; in some, we have policies without philosophy or program; in others, the program dominates both policy and philosophy.

Take first the issue of civil rights, especially as it relates to equality under the law. Our philosophy is beyond reproach. We hold that all persons are created equal, that all citizens of the United States are entitled to equal protection under the law. Yet our policies - some fixed into law - did not until recently come close to reflecting our philosophy. And even now, when policies have been brought closer to philosophy, principally because of Supreme Court decisions, programs to achieve the objectives of the policies fall short.

We have a policy about poverty in this country. Stated quite simply, the policy is to eliminate either poverty or the poor. The program to accomplish this is not only underfinanced, but it is based on a misconception of the nature and causes of poverty in the United States. We are still proceeding on Herbert Spencer's nineteenth-century philosophy that poverty is its own reward, and that poverty reflects faults that should not be encouraged by public help. Thus President Nixon in supporting his family-assistance program said that its basis was "workfare" and suggested, even though unemployment among the nonpoor was high, that the subtle motivation in his program would move the unemployed poor to go to work. The fact is that poverty is the result of a whole complex of causes - historical, psychological, economic, and cultural. Any great oversimplification or misconception of that reality can only result in failure of our efforts to deal with the problem of the poor in America. And. we are failing.

Our involvement in Vietnam was another case in point. The program there, namely military commitment, became the determinant of the policy. Tactics in the field determined strategy. As the program had become the policy, so the policy eventually became the philosophy, until President Nixon closed the circle by suggesting that we were fighting to secure the return of American prisoners of war and the evacuation of American troops. The consequences of the war, and of the policy leading to the war, were thus presented as causes and justifications for it.

The moon program, even more clearly than the Vietnam war, illustrates program making policy, even though it has not yet generated philosophy. President Kennedy, when explaining one reason for manned flights to the moon, quoted the mountain climber who said, "Because it is there."[92] President Johnson continued the program.

After the first flight had been successfully completed, it was said that the prestige of America abroad had been greatly enhanced and that morale at home was at a new high, or at least at a different level. Later flights were justified on scientific and economic grounds. The first flight report was that the moon was a dead planet. Subsequent flight reports added to this information by indicating that the moon was deader than it had been believed to be, and not only that, but that it had been dead longer than it had been believed to be dead. In truth, the scientific and technological fallout was limited principally to knowledge of how the human body behaves in a vacuum, and the economic fallout has been trivial.

Finally, there are the automobile and the highway building program: the fusion of technology, program, policy, and philosophy. Now we find the automobile, like the dinosaur, consuming its own environment, including its creators.

---

[92] *Public Papers of the Presidents: John F. Kennedy, 1962* (Washington, 1963), p. 671, address on the space effort, September 12, 1962. (Mr. Kennedy attributed the remark to the British explorer George Mallory.)

Meanwhile the highway building goes on - linking one congested city with another, one community with inadequate medical facilities with another having the same inadequacies, one polluted area with another. And the highway trust fund is treated as though it were the sacred money of the temple.

What we must do is step back, reexamine our philosophy, whether it be of things as basic as individual rights or as pragmatic, even transient, as the automobile. We must decide what we are and where we are going, set policies with those goals in mind, and then plan and develop programs to move us toward the goals we have set. The alternative is to surrender to process and, beyond that, to ignorance and false fear.

Trouble in the Economics Community

The liberal and the conservative schools of economics are challenging each other's theories, interpretations, and projections. Within the separate schools, especially within the liberal one, there is disagreement that falls somewhere between anarchy and civil war.

More serious than the disagreements is the fact that economists are questioning their own discipline. The width and depth of this questioning was reflected in six articles in the January 22, 1972, issue of Saturday Review under the title, "Does Economics Ignore You?"

The first of the six articles was by Leonard Silk, economics writer for *The New York Times*. He opened his article with a convenient quotation from Edmund Burke: "The age of chivalry is gone. That of the sophisters, economists, and calculators has succeeded; and the glory of Europe is extinguished for ever."[93] Seeming to approve Burke's judgment, Silk then asked in his own name, "But is the age of the economists already come to an end?"[94] He did not give a clear answer to the question but went on to say that the methodology of conventional economics, which he defined as the science of choice, was inadequate. He suggested that economists needed a deeper

---

[93] Edmund Burke, Reflections on the Revolution in France (Los Angeles, 1955 [originally published in 1790]), p. 111.

[94] Leonard Silk, "Wanted: A More Human, Less Dismal Science," *Saturday Review*, January 22, 1972, p. 35.

understanding of many matters that lie beyond the boundaries of conventional economics. Yet he also suggested that economics might disappear before it had proved itself even within the limits of its own defined competence.

Mr. Silk was followed by Daniel Fusfeld, of the University of Michigan, who did not see economics as disappearing but as in serious trouble. He started his analysis at least two stages beyond the stage at which President Nixon said he had arrived. Economics, Fusfeld said, was post-post-Keynesian. The thrust of Fusfeld's article was that the synthesis of the macroeconomics of John Maynard Keynes with the microeconomics of Alfred Marshall and his followers - the synthesis taught by Paul Samuelson and others - had been shattered. The synthesis had now become the thesis and had to be challenged. In concluding his article, Mr. Fusfeld, sounding more like a presidential candidate than an economist, declared that "the problems of the present indicate the path to the future"[95] and called for establishment of a humane economy on a worldwide scale.

The next entrant, starting in the third position, was Robert Lekachman of New York State University at Stony Brook. Mr. Lekachman analyzed Phase II of President Nixon's economic program in terms of what it showed about who controls the economy of this country and how they control it, and to what ends. He concluded, quite rightly in my opinion, that unless economists were to take into account the realities of who controls and who makes major policy decisions about the economy, their discipline would become less and less relevant.

As evidence of the rightness of his judgment, I cite the almost uncritical acceptance by the Congress of Phase II's first pay board, made up of Big Business, Big Labor, and Big Government (the last labeled public representation). Operating with slight constitutional or statutory authority, the board contained two elements of classical fascist government: Big Labor and Big Business. The third element, Big Military, was indirectly and partially represented through a few members.

Incidentally, there is little reason to believe that if any one of the three forces had emerged as predominant, the

---

[95] Daniel R. Fusfeld, "Post-Post-Keynes: The Shattered Synthesis," ibid., p. 39.

economic policies of the country would be significantly different.

Starting in gate four was Marc Roberts of Harvard. Mr. Roberts opened up all questions of philosophy in the third, fourth, and fifth sentences of his article when he asked: "Do people always know exactly what they 'really' want, no matter how complex the options? Will people always choose what makes them 'happiest' or 'best off? Are individual choices effectively immune from outside influence and manipulation?"[96] Economic theory, he said, is built on the assumption that there are simple and clear answers to each of these questions. Then he said that there are no simple and clear answers, that human responses cannot be predicted with the accuracy suggested by traditional economics.

Implicit in his position was the idea that we can no longer avoid intellectual and moral decisions about production, distribution, and consumption by escaping into a pseudoscience. We must face up to these problems in the real world of individual and social decision.

The fifth participant in the series was Robert Solo of Michigan State. He said that the trouble with economics was that it had been mathematized and that consequently its concepts had been placed beyond the test of reality. Since some of his fellow contributors said there was no real certainty about the concepts even before they were mathematized, it would seem that the trouble was not in mathematizing them but in attributing certainty and objectivity to them. Mathematizing them could only compound the error.

Solo concluded with the observation that economics, being outdated, "is, after all, very much in tune with the times."[97]

The sixth piece was by Charles Schultze, who was Budget Bureau Director under President Johnson and is now, as they say, "of the Brookings Institution." (Why some organizations are called Institutes, like Carnegie, and others are called Institutions, like Smithsonian and Brookings, is not clear. But "Institution" does sound more certain, more permanent, and more absolute. Why Mr. Schultze is "of" and not "with" the Institution raises another question. The explanation may be theological.

---

[96] Marc J. Roberts, "An Unsimple Matter of Choice," ibid., p. 46.

[97] Robert A. Solo, "New Maths and Old Sterilities," ibid., p. 48.

Angels, for example, are "of" a particular choir - of the Cherubim or the Seraphim; they are not "with" it, as a violinist might be said to be with the New York Philharmonic.)

In any case, Mr. Schultze was still for economics. But speaking somewhat sadly, much as G. K. Chesterton did when he said that Christianity had not failed but had not been tried, Schultze said that economics was not obsolete but rather underemployed.

We must acknowledge the weaknesses of economic theory as noted by the economists writing for Saturday Review. We have known that there were limits to economics as a science since economists first began to write about the economics of imperfect competition. And we have known that the value of economics as an applied science was significantly reduced with the development and application of Pavlovian psychology and high-pressure advertising. Other forces, principally political ones, have also impinged upon economics.

Today economics is about one part economic theory, one part individual and social psychology, and one part politics. Economics is still useful, but its limitations must be recognized.

What are we to do? Certainly we must take a new and hard look at economic problems. All of them have become worse since the Saturday Review writers looked at economic theory in 1972. Over twenty million Americans are still poor. Over seven million are out of work, and several million more are underemployed. A major recession is accompanied by a rate of inflation which has particularly serious effects on the poor, the unemployed, and those living on fixed incomes. President Ford has referred to inflation as taxation without representation. It would be more accurate to call it taxation with mismanagement.

Mismanagement did not begin with the Ford administration. At least since 1967, inflation has not been under control. Politicians were misled by the overoptimism and misjudgments of economists about such things as the supposedly inevitable growth of national production and the potential of the "peace increment." Politicians were also misled by their own misjudgments and false optimism about the costs and the duration of militarism and of the war in Vietnam. Consequently, they allowed the forces of inflation to go almost uncontrolled and undirected. Businessmen and bankers and financial managers generally went along with the same misjudgments and irresponsibility.

The American phase of the war in Vietnam was fought largely on credit. There was rather wild expansion of credit by nongovernmental institutions during the same period. To a large extent, the irresponsible extension of credit - both public and private - has resulted in our present pattern of economic disorders.

Beyond that, our economy now operates in a world in which we no longer control our own currency. During John Connally's short term as Secretary of the Treasury, he was hailed as the man who released the dollar by devaluation. In fact, this is an easy thing to do; it is like cutting the anchor rope. What it really meant was that we lost control or did not want to do what was necessary to help stabilize the dollar as a force in the free-trade area.

In addition to all this, we now have the unstabilizing force of the so-called petrodollars, which are turned into the free market almost every day by the oil countries.

We must answer for our failure to take into account three things. First, agricultural prices were depressed during most of the years after World War II and consequently offset inflation in other areas. This was like a special tax on the farmers. If they had received parity during those years, food costs would have been higher.

Second, too much oil and gasoline was provided and consumed in the face of declining supplies and in the face of the potential for higher prices that might be set either by economics or by politics. This encouraged the production and purchase of the wrong kind of automobiles and the building of the wrong kind of cities. It also encouraged industry to produce inefficiently or to use fuel inefficiently. One cannot blame the oil companies alone for this situation; one must also blame government and society for failing to make rational decisions about the use of oil and gasoline.

Third, because of the overoptimism of economists and politicians and businessmen, too much credit was supplied or created at interest rates that were too low. Many businesses have become so dependent on credit that they cannot stop borrowing, even when interest rates are quite high. It is like taking dope; they are hooked.

The current inflation does not meet the classical definition of too few goods being pursued by too much money. Rather - with the exception of food, which is in short supply - it is a case of too little money available to meet current needs, because what might be available has been pledged in payment for war and wasteful production of the past. So it is not available to pay for oil - the supply of which is limited by political decision - and for other goods and services, most of which are in adequate supply, if not in surplus.

Some short-term solutions for our economic problems may be helpful. But in the long run, we must answer for the cheap money, cheap food, and cheap oil that we have used so freely. The American economy is not like a speedboat; it cannot be turned around quickly or arbitrarily. It is more like an ocean liner whose course must be calculated and set well in advance.

At least eight things should be done to provide both short-term and long-term improvement of the economy:

-We should have limited and conditional wage/price controls.

-We should have selective credit controls, so that the limited supply of credit will be directed to meet social needs and to relieve the most critical inflationary pressures.

-We should have selective excise taxes to discourage wasteful production and consumption.

Proven devices such as investment credit and accelerated depreciation should be used selectively.

The Federal Reserve Board should be made at least partially subject to Treasury policy, instead of retaining its independence. The White House and the Congress have often used the Federal Reserve to cover their own irresponsibility. When they have refused to act against inflation by increasing taxes or reducing the budget, the Federal Reserve has tried to stem the tide with higher interest rates - a method that is not very effective because of the extreme expansion of credit and the mishandling of money and credit over the years. We should make the Federal Reserve responsible to the Treasury Department, and thus make the executive branch truly responsible for economic policy.

We should eliminate unnecessary expenditures in the military budget. In 1974 Senator Barry Goldwater estimated that the military budget could be reduced by five billion dollars. Given Senator Goldwater's background, that can only be viewed as a conservative estimate.

We should reduce government spending in some other areas, such as the space program and the highway-building program.

We must eliminate waste in the nongovernmental economy. This means, particularly, action against the waste and harm which the automobile as an institution causes in our economy and in our culture. Our cars are too big and too heavy; they take too much space, too much material, too much fuel. They cost too much, pollute too much, and kill too many people. Selective excise taxes and positive regulation of size, weight, speed, and fuel consumption can help reduce the great waste of money and life caused by the automobile.

Inflation and other disorders of our economy are not beyond solution as long as we have our great productive capacity. But we must make orderly and rational decisions about the use of our resources, about how we finance the operation of our economy, and about how we distribute work and income.

We do not need a revolution of rising expectations. We need one of moderating expectations - and of responsible management of the economy.

The President of the United States need not be his own Secretary of State. He should be his own economist.

Constitutional Amendments

Since the turn of the century, we have amended the Constitution of the United States too often. There were only four amendments to the Constitution in the 1800s; there have been eleven amendments so far in this century.

Some of the twentieth-century amendments were passed to remedy weaknesses in the Constitution.

Others, however, indicated timidity or a failure to understand the Constitution.

The Sixteenth Amendment, adopted in 1913, authorized the income tax. A good case can be made that the income tax was constitutional before the amendment was passed.

The Seventeenth Amendment, also adopted in 1913, provided for the direct election of senators. Many states were already on the way to adopting this procedure when the amendment was passed.

The Eighteenth Amendment, which took effect in 1920, was the Prohibition Amendment. It should never have been adopted, a fact recognized by its later repeal.

The Nineteenth Amendment, ratified in 1920, was the women's suffrage amendment. It should not have been needed, since the principle was already in the Constitution. But many of the states had been slow to act on the principle.

Since adoption of the Nineteenth Amendment, the states have been slow to guarantee equal rights to women in employment and other areas. This has made necessary the Equal Rights Amendment, which was proposed by Congress in 1972 and sent to the states, where, after several years, it eventually failed to gain approval by those legislatures.

The Twentieth Amendment, adopted in 1933, corrected a few minor mistakes or omissions in the Constitution. For example, it reduced the lame-duck periods for President and Congress.

The Twenty-first Amendment, which repealed Prohibition, was also adopted in 1933.

The Twenty-second Amendment, ratified in 1951, barred anyone from serving more than two terms as President. It was adopted by way of getting even with Franklin D. Roosevelt after he died. As a consequence of this amendment, Presidents have begun to think they have a right to a second term because it will necessarily be their last term. Yet at the same time they think, "I have to be careful until my second term." So for four years there is a kind of holding action in the White House. It is a prescription for two irresponsible presidential terms: the first because the principal concern is to be elected to the second, and the second because one is no longer answerable to the electorate. The Nixon administrations are an example of this danger.

The Twenty-third Amendment was ratified in 1961. It gave the District of Columbia a voice in electing the President and Vice President. But local self-government is more important to the District than the right to vote for President. The Congress finally realized this in 1973, when it allowed the District a limited form of home rule.

The Twenty-fourth Amendment, ratified in 1964, outlawed the poll tax in federal elections. This amendment was unnecessary; it was passed as a sort of consolation to the South. State poll taxes imposed in federal elections could have been outlawed by statute.

The Twenty-fifth Amendment deals with presidential disability and succession; it was ratified in 1967. Most of the problems in this area could have been dealt with by statute. But a more serious objection is that the amendment makes possible a basic conflict between President and Vice President, since it gives the Vice President a role in deciding whether or not the President is disabled. A President could claim he is fit to exercise the duties of his office, while the Vice President claims he is not and seeks to win over the Cabinet against him. This would be something like the time when there was one claimant to the papacy in Rome and another in Avignon, or the long period when there was dispute over the English crown. And even if a Vice President were sincere in believing the President disabled, he would always be subject to suspicion as to motive.

Another part of the Twenty-fifth Amendment provides for filling a vacancy in the office of Vice President. This was first used in 1973 after the resignation of Spiro Agnew, then again in 1974 after Gerald Ford succeeded to the presidency.

The Twenty-sixth and latest amendment was adopted in 1971. It granted suffrage to eighteen-year-olds - a deserving amendment in itself, but one which was supported by some to compensate or make up for the abuse of young people in the 1960s.

While much attention was given to the amendments described above, several constitutional problems of greater significance were neglected. They do not necessarily require amendments, but they do require attention.

The first is the importance of foreign policy today as contrasted with its importance at the time the Constitution was adopted. The men who drafted the Constitution clearly had in mind a United States that would stand somewhat apart from the rest of the world. This was a reasonable judgment on their part. There were limitations of travel and communication at the time which isolated the United States from other countries. The thrust of our nation was westward; the concern was with expansion on our own continent. The founding fathers had no reason to believe that we would become a great world power.

The drafters of the Constitution assumed that the Senate could exercise sufficient influence on foreign policy if it had the authority to accept or reject nominations for Secretary of State and ambassadors and if it had similar authority over treaties. Most foreign policy was conducted by treaty in the early days of the Republic. Today, however, we generally have treaties only if they cover something like outer space or the Antarctic. The fewer people an area has, the easier it is to get a treaty for it. More significant policies often are set by executive agreements that are not submitted to the Senate for approval. Consequently, the Senate in recent years has spent much time in trying to catch up with executive agreements and trying to insist on its constitutional duty to give advice on foreign policy.

A second problem the founding fathers did not anticipate was the development of great military power in this country. Their concept of the military went no further than temporary armies in time of war. Instead we now have a permanent and very powerful military establishment, one that is not always firmly controlled by elected officials.

A third change that has occurred since adoption of the Constitution is the growth of the judiciary. Originally the judiciary was conceived as being made up of many local courts, with an ultimate appeal to the Supreme Court. But we have since moved toward a truly national judicial system.

In the past ten or fifteen years, however, we have gone beyond the natural growth of the national court system. We have placed an extra burden on the courts by permitting them or forcing them to run ahead of both the executive and legislative branches of the government. Significant court decisions on civil rights go back at least to 1944, but there was no comprehensive, twentieth-century legislation on civil rights until 1964. More recently, class-action suits have asked the courts to effect social reform in this country - in some cases without executive support, in other cases with little or no statutory and financial support.

The fourth and last major development not anticipated by the Constitution is the role of political parties. This development has been extraconstitutional; much of it has been haphazard. At times there has been no order, no equity, no justice, and very little reason in the way political parties have operated in this country. And the legislative underwriting of the two-party system, including legislative discrimination against independent candidates and new parties, may well be unconstitutional.

Constitutional change may be needed to meet some of the problems not anticipated by the founding fathers. But such problems as the erosion of Senate power in foreign policy and of congressional authority over the military can be met in large part by a return to the procedures set forth in the Constitution.

Five Systems of Justice

Nearly twenty-five years ago we passed the two hundredth anniversary of a year in which several meetings of significance were held. The participants were not exactly law-and-order men, nor did they consider themselves members of a silent majority. As a consequence of their meetings, the Declaration of Independence was written and made public. It asserted that all men are created equal and that they have unalienable rights of life, liberty, and the pursuit of happiness.

The men who drafted that document were not engaged in a rhetorical exercise; they were not detached political philosophers. They were practical politicians who were playing for keeps. Their property, their reputations, and their lives were on the line. But they had principles. They had a policy designed to realize those principles and then a program - first the Revolution and then the Constitution - to carry out the policy.

Over two hundred years later, we are called upon to assess how far we have come toward the goals and ideals which the Declaration and the Constitution set for our country.

By 1972 we had come from George Washington to Richard Nixon, from John Adams to Spiro Agnew, from Alexander Hamilton to John Connally, and from Edmund Randolph to John Mitchell. We should ask some questions about what happened along the way and how much progress of that kind the country can stand.

The record on liberty and justice suggests that we have a long way to go. The ancient Romans were more honest than we. They admitted that they had two systems of justice. We say that we have one, but in fact we do not. We have at least five different systems of justice.

First is the ideal one, the one we like to talk about. This is the one in which constitutional guarantees are recognized; due process is not just an abstract right but a reality. This is the system we believe in. It does exist and operate for many Americans. They must have status, money, and one or two other qualifications.

There is a second system of justice for the poor, for members of racial minorities, for the young people of this country, for those who challenge established positions. This is the system of preventive detention and protective custody. It is the system of wiretapping and of bugging protest groups and people like the late Martin Luther King, Jr. This is the system in which the military kept confidential files on millions of civilians, including certain black leaders and certain antiwar senators. In this system there is a different bill of rights. There is a different concept of the right of privacy, the right of habeas corpus, freedom of assembly, freedom of speech, and freedom of the press.

There is a third system of justice which is applied to those who administer justice in the second system. The third system was applied to Chicago policemen after the 1968 Democratic convention and to Mississippi policemen after the shootings at Jackson State College in 1970. Its operating principle seems to be that justice is different for those who act in the name of the state than for other persons.

The fourth system of justice is that of our military establishment. It has many of the same contradictions and inequities that are found in the civilian order. The fourth system punished a lieutenant for the My Lai massacre. It allowed a general who conducted unauthorized bombing raids in Vietnam to retire with no court-martial, only a slight reduction of rank, and full retirement pay. While this occurred, the Commander in Chief was campaigning for re-election and promising that he would make young draft evaders "pay a price"[98] for their action.

A fifth system, of limited application to persons of high political office such as Presidents and Vice Presidents - developed after Watergate.

This is the state of justice in America. What should we do about it?

We have two choices. We can accept, as the Romans did, that justice is a different thing for different kinds of people. Or we can move toward one system of justice for all Americans.

---

[98] *Public Papers of the Presidents: Richard M. Nixon, 1972*
(Washington, 1974), p. 987, remarks to meeting of National League of Families of American Prisoners and Missing in Southeast Asia, October 16, 1972.

Due process is basic to every right of citizenship and every principle in the Declaration of Independence and the Constitution. If we wish to secure it for all, we should remember that it is more than a matter of equal treatment. It is the insistence that everyone in our society be treated finally and most completely as a person.

The Enemies List

On Wednesday, June 27,1973, John W. Dean III, by then a former White House aide, presented to the Senate Select Committee on Presidential Campaign Activities (generally known as the Ervin Committee) documents from a file called "Opponents List and Political Enemies Project." According to Dean, the list was first compiled in the office of Mr. Charles Colson while the latter was Special Counsel to President Nixon. The list was sent to Dean in the summer of 1971. Other White House staff members added many names to the list, which eventually included over two hundred people. It has become known as the Enemies List and is made up of the names of persons and organizations judged by Mr. Colson and others to be unfriendly, if not dangerous, to the Nixon administration and, therefore, to be given special attention. A Dean memorandum suggested how to deal with the enemies.

Response has been mixed. Some of the persons on the list thought it a great joke. Others saw it as an alarming threat to individual liberty. The response of political columnists and commentators ranged from those who dismissed it as irresponsible to those who described it, as Hans J. Morgenthau[99] did, as a part of "The Aborted Nixon Revolution." William F. Buckley, Jr., wrote:

Dean's memorandum was an act of proto-fascism. It is altogether ruthless in its dismissal of human rights. It is fascist in its reliance on the state as the instrument of harassment. It is fascist in its automatic assumption that the state in all matters comes before the right of the individual. And it is fascist in tone: The stealth, the brutality, the self-righteousness. It is far and away the

---

[99] Hans J. Morgenthau in *The New Republic*, August 11, 1973, pp. 17 19.

most hideous document to have come out of the Watergate investigation.[100]

How seriously should the list and its accompanying commentary be taken? Out of context, the list has amusing aspects. How else could one look upon a list that included Carol Channing as an enemy of the state? Or Joe Namath?

If you assume that the enemies were to be treated as proposed in the Dean memorandum, it might be desirable to be on it. Inclusion would set you free from many bothersome details of life. For example, if you knew that your income tax would be audited, you could simply send all your records of income and expenditures to the Internal Revenue Service. They could keep the records. You would need no bookkeeper or accountant. At the end of the year IRS could settle the balance, and you would feel perfectly secure. If this service had been available generally and had been used by President Nixon, he would have avoided many tax problems.

If you were sure that your telephone would be tapped, you could do without an answering service, possibly even without a secretary; you could dictate directly into the phone and then ask the recording agency to give you a copy of the tape or even a transcript. The telephone company would certainly keep your phone in order, and if you moved, you would not have to wait long for installation of a new phone.

If you knew that your files would be rifled, you might anticipate that they would be left in better alphabetical order than had been the case before the rifling.

The police protection would also be very helpful. How reassuring it would be if you took a little walk in New York or Washington, or if you made the run from your parked car to your apartment door, to know that secret agents were close at hand.

If all these advantages followed from being on the list, other citizens might sue for inclusion, using the constitutional guarantee of equal protection under the law as a basis for class action. Eventually the list would be expanded to include all citizens, and democracy could start over again in America.

---

[100] William F. Buckley, Jr., in *National Review*, August 3, 1973, p. 859.

In fact, if one considers the purposes for which the list was drawn and the methods proposed to accomplish its objectives, the list is far from amusing.

"Punishing one's enemies and rewarding one's friends" is an expression known to American politics. But "enemies" in this context usually has been a term applied to persons active in politics. Reward has meant patronage - possible appointment to the office of postmaster, ambassadorships, other limited preferences. Punishment usually has meant the denial of similar favors, all within the limits of accepted political practice. The Nixon staff's list of enemies was quite different, both as to those included and as to the means of punishment.

First, it refined the political classification by setting up categories such as "Black Congressmen." It also included many persons who were not directly involved in politics: journalists, businessmen, celebrities, academics, and even whole organizations.

More serious than the extension of the list were the methods proposed for dealing with the enemies in John Dean's memorandum of August 16, 1971. The "fact of our incumbency,"[101] that is, the occupancy of the White House - and with that the control over the executive agencies of the government - was to be maximized in dealing with persons on the list. Attention was to be given to "how we can use the available federal machinery to screw our political enemies."[102]

As to means and methods on the negative side, grants and federal contracts might be denied. But there was also emphasis on positive action - by litigation and prosecution. (A separate briefing paper for H. R. Haldeman suggested how the Internal Revenue Service could be made "politically responsive."[103]) This positive methodology becomes more disturbing if we look at the recommendations for dealing with persons selected for special and concentrated attention:

Ed Guthman, an editor of the *Los Angeles Times* - "It is time to give him the message."[104]

---

[101] U.S. Senate, *Hearings Before the Select Committee on Presidential Campaign Activities ... Phase I: Watergate Investigation*, Book 4, p. 1689, memorandum from John W. Dean III, August 16, 1971.

[102] ibid.

[103] ibid., p. 1682, briefing paper prepared for H. R. Haldeman.

[104] ibid., p. 1694, list titled "Opponent Priority Activity".

Maxwell Dane, of the advertising firm of Doyle Dane Bernbach - "They should be hit hard starting with Dane."[105]

Ruth Picker and David Picker, of United Artists Corporation - "should be programmed..."[106]

Morton Halperin, of Common Cause "A scandal would be most helpful here."[107]

The punishments, it is indicated, were to cover the range of human ambitions and aspirations: material well-being to be taken care of by denial of contracts and grants; power to be denied, especially for those in politics but also for those in advertising and in the media; self-esteem, reputation, perhaps pride to be wounded by public disgrace, by prosecutions, by scandal, and for the select, as Haldeman suggested, by the ultimate denial of not being invited to White House dinners and receptions.

One must hesitate to draw comparisons between any event and historical Nazism. Because of the incomprehensible horror of that experience in Western civilization, comparison never helps very much. The metaphorical use or example always overwhelms the reality to which it is compared. But one can make comparison of methods without suggesting that their application would have led to the same things that marked Nazism in Germany. This limited comparison is not only defensible but clearly called for.

The staff of the Senate Subcommittee on Constitutional Rights observed in its 1972 report on Army surveillance of civilians:

What separates military intelligence in the United States from its counterparts in totalitarian states, then, is not its capabilities, but its intentions. This is a significant distinction but one which may not wholly reassure many Americans who rely on a government of laws and not of the intentions of men, no matter how honorable.[108]

---

[105] ibid.

[106] ibid.

[107] ibid.

[108] U.S. Senate, Committee on the Judiciary, Subcommittee on Constitutional Rights, staff report, *Army Surveillance of Civilians* (Washington, 1972), p. 96.

Intentions can change very quickly. Sometimes it is best not to have available the capacity to achieve the objectives of changing intentions.

William L. Shirer, in his book The Rise and Fall of the Third Reich, stated accurately that "the Third Reich owed nothing to the fortunes of war or to foreign influence. It was inaugurated in peacetime, and peacefully, by the Germans themselves, out of both their weaknesses and their strengths."[109] On January 30, 1933, President Hindenburg, following constitutional procedures, made Adolf Hitler Chancellor of Germany, with the responsibility of organizing a government Hitler decided almost immediately to dissolve the Reichstag and hold new elections, with the executive powers of the government controlled principally by the Nazi party. "Now it will be easy," Joseph Goebbels[110], Nazi propaganda leader, wrote in his diary on February 3, 1933, "to carry on the fight, for we can call on all the resources of the State. Radio and press are at our disposal. We shall stage a masterpiece of propaganda. And this time, naturally, there is no lack of money."

"...all the resources of the State" wrote Goebbels in 1933; "...the available federal machinery..." wrote John Dean in our time.

"...naturally, there is no lack of money" - Goebbels, 1933; "...you could get a million dollars[111]. And you could get it in cash..." President Nixon said in 1973 when considering money for a cover-up of Watergate.

In February 1933 German big businessmen were called to a meeting at Hermann Goring's Reichstag President's Palace. Dr. Hjalmar Schacht was the host. Among those who came were representatives of Krupp and I. G. Farben. Hitler spoke. He would eliminate the Marxists and restore the Wehrmacht; he would remain in power regardless of the election outcome. Some years later at Nuremberg, Dr. Schacht reported that he had collected three million marks at the meeting.

---

[109] William L. Shirer, The Rise and Fall of the Third Reich (New York, 1960), p. 187.

[110] quoted in ibid., p. 189.

[111] U.S. House of Representatives, Committee on the Judiciary, *Transcripts of Eight Recorded Presidential Conversations* (Washington, 1974), p. 94, comment by Mr. Nixon in meeting with H. R. Haldeman and John W. Dean III, March 21,1973.

In 1971 and early 1972 Maurice Stans, formerly a Secretary of Commerce, talked to businessmen. At his urging or on their own, they came, some with money in suitcases, some with checks on foreign banks, some with their own money, some with money taken illegally from corporate funds (American Airlines, Gulf Oil, Minnesota Mining, and others), some wanting favorable action on cases pending before the Justice Department or regulatory agencies, some wanting no more than ambassadorships, some just wanting to be sure.

The threat of Communism was emphasized by the Nazis in 1933. In the United States in 1971 and 1972, national security was the justification for Watergate and related activities.

On March 23, 1933, the Reichstag passed the Enabling Act, taking the power of legislation including that over the Reich budget and the approval of treaties, as well as other powers away from the parliament and giving it to the executive branch. In our time, the President of the United States asserted that he was autonomous in the field of foreign policy and that, as Commander in Chief, he could order the Cambodian invasion and the bombing of Vietnam and Laos. And the President declared his right not to administer programs approved and financed by the Congress.

In Germany in 1933, not trusting the regular police, Hermann Goring set up his own secret police. In 1971, not trusting the FBI or the CIA to do their work, President Nixon set up his own White House secret investigative force called the "plumbers."

What followed in Germany scarcely needs repeating. There were lists of people to be purged. In the early days they were named; later race alone was sufficient to qualify for the list. We had our enemies list and various national security causes. Illegal breaking and entering, spying, wiretapping, potential blackmail, and campaign sabotage followed.

We must ask and try to answer the question of why these things could happen. They were more than a projection of the character of Richard Nixon, although many of the things carried on by the Committee for the Re-election of the President were not very different from things that he had approved in some of his previous political campaigns.

Members of the Committee for the Re-election of the President and the White House aides most directly involved in the 1972 campaign seemed to be of one mind about the methods to be used, and equal in their dedication to the cause.

The loyalty of the President's closest supporters and confidants was unquestioning, and his association with them covered many years. When he tried to disassociate himself from many activities of the campaign, it was fair to ask why he had gathered around him so many persons who seemed not to understand what kind of campaign he wanted, or why they seemed insensitive to what he expected of them.

Perhaps their conduct can be explained as a manifestation of the urge to remain in what C. S. Lewis described as the Inner Ring. The Inner Ring, as I have mentioned before, is a group exempted from rules that apply to others. The members of the group have a special sense of belonging. One might say that the temptation of the Inner Ring caused the fall of the angels and has since worked down to our level.

Beyond the Inner Ring, support for the President came principally from two definable and somewhat different kinds of persons: the Liddy, Hunt, McCord, Barker, Gray group on the one hand, and the Strachan, Porter, Magruder group on the other. The motivation of the first group was rather obvious. They were doing what came naturally to them, or what they were conditioned or trained to do. They were patriots. They were worried about subversion; most of them were trained and experienced as spies. The methodology of Watergate and lists of enemies were things they understood. James McCord drew the line when he discovered that his old love and first loyalty, the CIA, was to be exploited. The breaking point for L. Patrick Gray was somewhere between his assertion of integrity and admission of falsification.

The motivations and justifications of the second group were less clear. Long time association with the President was not the mark of their relationship. They were not trained in dirty tricks. They did not appear to be intense and worried superpatriots. They may well be a new breed of political mercenaries, calculating the best way to make it and then doing what is necessary. Certainly in 1972 the Republican game was the best one going.

The contrast in the moral or ethical justifications offered by the two groups is interesting. The first group seemed to rely on the classical ethical argument of the greater good as justifying a lesser evil for example, lying to save a life or to save a country or perhaps even to save an administration. Jeb Stuart Magruder argued from the teachings and examples of modern moralists, citing in particular William Sloane Coffin, Jr., as being at least in part responsible for his actions. His was a case of situation ethics. Starting from different premises and using different systems of ethics, both groups justified essentially the same acts.

There is some evidence that in the second group the desire to make the Inner Ring or, failing in that, to overleap it or bypass it, was a strong force. By good service, by anticipating the President's desires, there must have been a hope of receiving recognition, somewhat in the same manner as in T. S. Eliot's <u>Murder in the Cathedral</u> when the knights, anticipating the wishes of the king, murdered Thomas A Becket, or as in Shakespeare's Richard III when Sir James Tyrrel, the lesser nobleman, proved his loyalty to the king by arranging the murder of the young princes.

Charles Péguy, in reflecting on a certain period of history, said that it had been the historic role of the Germans at that time to reveal the mind of evil before it had the capacity to achieve all its objectives. It may well be that Watergate and the enemies list are clear warnings of where we have been going. These warnings should make us examine the practices, attitudes, and ideas that have infected our political and governmental processes. We have come very close to the condition described by the Duke in Shakespeare's <u>Measure for Measure</u>. In response to the question, "What news abroad in the world?" the Duke said: "There is scarce truth enough alive to make societies secure, but security enough to make fellowships accursed. Much upon this riddle runs the wisdom of the world."[112]

Censorship

---

[112] William Shakespeare, <u>Measure for Measure</u>, Act 111, scene ii.

Most discussion of censorship in recent times has dealt with efforts to limit or halt the use of pornographic material after it has been produced.

More serious in a democracy is the selection and control of political information and ideas before they are even spoken or published.

Who determines what persons shall speak and write, since not everyone can speak or write? Who selects what is to be recorded and transmitted to others, since not everything can be recorded?

There is danger in the concentrated control of television and radio stations; danger, too, in government efforts to regulate broadcasting. There is danger in concentrated ownership of newspapers and some danger in the development of nationally syndicated columnists. There is danger in standardized education and in the concentration of selection by book publishers and reviewers.

All these problems require serious attention. Some of them can be alleviated by private initiative. For example, the journalism reviews now published by some reporters provide standards by which to judge the press.

The problem of government control over information seems more dangerous and more difficult to counter. In the name of national security, the government justifies the withholding of almost any item of information and, beyond that, even the making of false statements.

The problem of government control was intensified during the Eisenhower administration, in part because many of its appointees were drawn from big business and from the military. The procedures of those institutions are not democratic, nor are they ordinarily conducted with the safeguards of the Constitution. Neither of them has anything comparable to the "balance of powers" concept.

Consequently, the Eisenhower administration took on many aspects of a corporate military structure. The President and his Cabinet resembled the top executives of a corporation or the high officers of a military establishment. They set policy and administered it largely on their own initiative; they resisted external review.

The Congress was treated very much like a corporate board of directors, or junior military officers occasionally gathered for a briefing, given permission to ask a few questions, but not necessarily given full answers. Congressional recommendations were politely received and conveniently filed away. The general understanding was that the senior officers had more complete knowledge and thus were in a better position to determine policy.

The people, of course, were at the lowest level of the structure. They were comparable to corporate stockholders or army troops. The general policy toward them was to withhold information which might discourage them or might cause them to lose heart, and to tell them only those things likely to encourage optimism.

At the time it seemed that this model might be only a temporary departure from tradition. But subsequent administrations not only copied the Eisenhower model, they made it worse.

One official of the Kennedy administration suggested that news generation by the government "is part of the weaponry"[113]; he also suggested a government's right to lie. The Johnson administration withheld much significant information and distorted or even fabricated other information. The "credibility gap" became an everyday phrase to describe that administration.

The Nixon administration continued the pattern. During President Nixon's first term, a Senate Foreign Relations subcommittee studied United States military commitments around the world. The subcommittee, chaired by Senator Stuart Symington of Missouri, encountered great difficulty in obtaining information from the administration. Even in cases where the administration provided information, it often insisted on deleting the information from the public transcript. Much of this censorship evidently had nothing to do with national security. Rather, it was used to avoid embarrassment to our government and to some foreign governments. The Nixon administration also gave false information to the Congress with reference to the bombing of Cambodia.

In 1971 Daniel Ellsberg released to major newspapers the documents known as the Pentagon Papers. These traced the development of American activity in Vietnam in great detail and proved deception of Americans by their government over a period of many years. Though the Nixon administration itself was not covered by the Pentagon Papers, it sought court orders to prevent *The*

---

[113] Arthur Sylvester, quoted in *The New York Times*, November 1, 1962, p. 17.

New York Times and *The Washington Post* from printing the papers.

It was not only the government that indicated a failure to understand the Bill of Rights on this occasion. *The New York Times* and the *Washington Post* retreated in the face of government pressure; they stopped printing the papers until the injunctions were overturned by the Supreme Court. They backed off and said in effect, "We hope the Court will save us." They thus weakened their claim to freedom of the press.

They also indicated a serious misunderstanding of that freedom. It is not a private right of newspapers. Essentially it is a matter of the public's right to knowledge and to truth. The newspapers did not have a right to withhold the truth from the people; they had an obligation to publish it. The press is responsible to the people, not to the government.

Recognition of this responsibility is essential to democracy. The press must stand as a defender of the people against large concentrations of power, including the power of government. In particular, the press must stand against the notion that the people cannot be trusted with information. If the people of a democracy are to make reasoned judgments, they must have the information on which such judgments can be based.

Part IV
A Good Person Is Not
So Hard to Find

John Bennett

John Coleman Bennett is a minister, theologian, and teacher. He served as Dean of Faculty and later as President of Union Theological Seminary. Dr. Bennett has written many articles and books, including Christians and the State and Foreign Policy in Christian Perspective.

When one speaks or writes in tribute to someone like John Bennett, one ordinarily begins by saying, "I remember the first time I met him" or "the first time I read him."

I cannot recall when either of these things happened. There was no first time. Somehow it seems that John Bennett has always been there, giving guidance and sustaining me in judgments that I made or thought I might have to make.

This has been my experience through some thirty years of reading him, both in and out of Christianity and Crisis. Thirty years ago we looked for a religious judgment on political questions. That was the direction of John Bennett's thought, and on many critical issues the thrust of religious judgment had significant effects.

It now seems that we have swung round and are more worried about the thrust of political judgment on our religious beliefs and on religious activity. John Bennett has been slow to join in that kind of judgment.

In every session of the Senate there is an amendment introduced to make the United States a religious country by constitutional decree - and even a Christian country. Twenty years ago the Congress required by law that American money carry the inscription, "In God We Trust." (Approval of the legislation was partly a vote of lack of confidence in the Secretary of the Treasury, and some hoped it might be anti-inflationary.) John Bennett has not supported such proposals.

More recently there was the question of whether students in the military academies should have to attend religious services. In an interesting justification of religion by politics, a ranking military officer said that an atheist could not be as great a military leader as a believer. John Bennett was not there to sustain that testimony.

But on the vital issues, John Bennett, more than anyone else, was there. He moved quickly to eliminate the irrelevant and to make clear that some historical differences and causes of conflict no longer existed or that they no longer had, if they ever did, any significance.

He did not concern himself only with the great issues, because he knew that sometimes disagreements on small issues can have consequences of great significance. He involved himself in the issue of aid to parochial schools. He was involved when we were worried whether the Democrats could elect a Catholic President. (More recently we have worried whether they can elect anybody.) Even on the question of an ambassador to the Vatican, he was concerned.

But it was not on these incidental and minor issues that John Bennett made his great contribution. It was on those issues that required a deep and fundamental moral judgment in American politics that his words were spoken and written and at least by some of us were heard.

From him, we received an early judgment and commitment against the war in Vietnam. And from him, we receive continuing judgment on subtle moral questions such as control over life through nuclear biology and other forms of advanced science.

We will remember what John Bennett has said and done in the past but also look forward to what he will say and do in the future.

Emerson Hynes

Emerson Hynes (1915-1971) taught sociology at St. John's University, Minnesota, for many years. He was my Legislative Assistant during the two terms I served in the United States Senate.

Emerson Hynes and I were students together. Later we were together on the faculty at St. John's University. For the last twelve years of his life, he was with me in the Senate as aide, counselor, and friend.

Emerson had a vocation to conversation. He was most appreciated by people with truly desperate causes. When persons in great distress, or with problems for which there was no political solution, came by the Senate office, he would never say, "Don't send them in to see me." Often the same persons would come to me later and say, "Thank you for letting us talk to that man."

Emerson brought to all problems a knowledge of history and a familiarity with philosophy. One did not start from scratch in discussing a problem with him. Few other members of the Senate, if any, had aides such as he to whom they could turn and ask, expecting an answer, "What did Plato [or Thomas Aquinas or Jacques Maritain] have to say about this?"

Father Emeric Lawrence, O.S.B., in his tribute to our friend, said that Emerson in his life was pleasing to God. I agree and would add that he was also pleasing to men. Sometimes the standards imposed by men are harder to satisfy than those imposed by God.

John Kennedy

John F. Kennedy (1917-1963) served in the House of Representatives and in the Senate before his election as President of the United States in 1960. He also had experience in journalism, and he received a Pulitzer Prize for his book Profiles in Courage.

In *Look* magazine in July 1963, Sidney Hyman wrote of trouble on the New Frontier:

A baffling dark breeze is now blowing through Washington's political community. No one knows for sure what whipped it up, what it portends or when it will pass away. The effects take many forms. There are murmurs of things that are vaguely wrong, of plans to set something vaguely right. But there are no prophets shouting. If any one speaker dominates the Washington scene, it is the professor who shows with charts why it is manly to seek only the possible and not the good - to let the part pass for the whole ... to make workability the proof of truth and usefulness the test of value.[114]

There were, to be sure, areas of failure in the Kennedy administration by late 1963 and much unfinished business. The overemphasis upon armaments and on the "missile gap" in the campaign of 1960 had set the country on a course of larger and larger military budgets, and perhaps had led to the invasion of Cuba, the subsequent missile confrontation, and the humiliation of Khrushchev, a humiliation which contributed significantly to his fall from power and to the suspension, if not the reversal, of the move to ease East West tensions.

With the advice and counsel of Dean Rusk, the Secretary of State, and of Robert McNamara, the Secretary of Defense, the President, in committing approximately sixteen thousand troops to Vietnam, had changed our involvement there in a quantitative way.

Whether he would have escalated the war as did President Johnson, no one can know. Some of his closest associates say that he would not have done so. There is

---

[114] Sidney Hyman, "Why There's Trouble on the New Frontier," *Look*, July 2, 1963, p. 30.

reason to believe that they are correct. President Kennedy did limit American participation in the Cuban venture and ended it without the showdown that some were urging on him. He might have been more responsive to early critics of the war, since most of the critics were closer to him both as persons and as politicians than they were to President Johnson.

The wisdom of the Kennedy administration's economic policies was reflected in rising production, a fall in unemployment, and a reasonably controlled rate of inflation.

The problems of the poor and of the chronically unemployed, however, were not met. Urban decay continued. Progress in civil rights was more a consequence of the execution of court decisions than it was a result of legislation recommended by the President and passed by the Congress. The major legislative record on civil rights was to be made later.

The personalization of the presidency, first as a matter of style and then as to procedures and substance, advanced. Carefulness and compromise in anticipation of the 1964 election more and more became the marks of the administration; the New Frontier became in some measure a rear guard action or holding operation.

But the spirit of America in 1963, the last year of the administration and of the life of John Kennedy, was one of optimism and hope. Quiet courage and civility had become the mark of American government. New programs of promise and dedication the Peace Corps, the Alliance for Progress had been presented and to some degree accepted, if not realized.

The promise of equal rights for all had been given, and a beginning toward the fulfillment of that promise had been made. What the continuation and flourishing of the good spirit released in John Kennedy's administration might have done for the nation remains an unanswered question.

Then came the trip to Dallas, and death. Political failure or partial failure has been forgotten as it should have been.

What is and should be remembered is the promise and style of John Kennedy and of his presidency. For he brought to that office a willingness to accept with good heart the burden and responsibility of citizenship. He brought the spirit of public happiness which possessed the

American colonists at the time of the Revolution and which was reflected in their delight in public discussion and public action, in joy of citizenship and civic commitment, in self government, in self discipline in a political community. Years later John Adams wrote: "The Revolution was effected before the war commenced. The Revolution was in the minds and hearts of the people..."[115]

John Kennedy brought to office a vision of the unity of Western civilization and, beyond that, the unity of all peoples of the world. He spoke of realizing the potential of all created things - a potential to be measured not by arithmetic or by geometric limits, but by the infinity of human aspirations and of human achievements in using the material resources of the earth to the limits of science.

And he urged upon us an effort to secure the fullest possible development of every person from the simple, and even the retarded, to those with the greatest talents encouraging everyone to seek the goal that he had set for himself and had described in the words, "the full use of your powers along lines of excellence."[116]

November 22, 1963, was a day out of season. It was a day both, it seemed, of spring and fall, both of beginnings and endings, but in the balance of time the ending has proved the stronger. What was changed was a something of the spirit. We have not yet recovered.

---

[115] John Adams, The Works of John Adams, ed. by Charles Francis Adams (Boston, 1856), Vol. X, p. 282, letter of February 13, 1818, to H. Niles.

[116] Public Papers of the Presidents: John F. Kennedy, 1963 (Washington, 1964), p. 644, remarks to students, August 27, 1963. Mr. Kennedy also used this definition on other occasions; he attributed it to the ancient Greeks.

Dan and Doris Kimball

Dan Kimball (1896-1970) was a businessman who served as Secretary of the Navy during the Truman administration. Among his many public concerns in later years was the development of a community-controlled corporation for the Watts area of Los Angeles. His wife, Doris Fleeson Kimball (1901-1970), was a reporter and columnist. She was also a founder of the American Newspaper Guild and a champion of women's rights. Dan Kimball died on July 30, 1970; Doris died two days later.

In medieval times the carvings on some doors carried these words: "When I consider life and death, I wonder why I am of such good cheer."

If we ask the same question while considering the lives of Dan Kimball and Doris Fleeson and their deaths, we must respond affirmatively, saying that we can be of some good cheer.

To write of them and to write well is not a very serious challenge. One need make no apologies. One need not speak with reservation. The only challenge is to present the integrity and the purity that marked the lives of these two persons.

Dan Kimball was an American, made by America and contributing to the making of America. A man of great optimism, he looked upon this world and found it good. He served his country's needs in war and also in peace. He looked upon business as a genuine profession, carrying with it personal privileges but also deep social obligations.

He was a dedicated Secretary of the Navy. In recent years, carrying that same sense of obligation, he responded to the special needs of this country: the needs of its poor and of its denied. He was among the first of those who said that we must take business and industry to the people. His project in Watts, I hope, will become a model for this nation. He did not stop with concern for domestic needs; his last great effort was that of establishing a technical university to meet the needs of the people of Morocco. This in brief was the public and private record of Dan Kimball.

Doris Fleeson looked upon this same world and found it good, but also judged that it could be made much better. So she considered it her calling in journalism to tell this world what was wrong with it, and who was wrong, and to suggest in terms that no one could misunderstand what she thought ought to be done.

She was the master of her profession. She knew the craft of writing but did not stop short at that mastery. She studied what it meant to be a reporter, spurning the background briefing, refusing to accept any special consideration because of her special talents or because of being a woman. Respect for the integrity of her craft and her profession marked her entire life.

These are the records of two persons in different fields, each deserving tribute and praise.

There was another aspect of their lives - that of their marriage and their life together. This living together was not a simple addition of two lives. It was not an arithmetical matter of one plus one. A very special condition, almost a new kind of person, emerged from their marriage. They did not manifest toward each other only compassion and respect but something more than that - a love of a deeper kind that can best be described as reverence. I can think of no words that come closer to describing that relationship than three lines from a poem by William Butler Yeats, in which he described a near perfect relationship of a man and a woman:

The hourly kindness, the day's common speech,
The habitual content of each with each
When neither soul nor body has been crossed.[117]

Those of us who knew either of these two persons separately were in a special way favored. Those of us who knew both of them, although separately, were doubly favored. Those of us who knew them together were most singularly blessed.

A theologian recently said that we do not know whither we go or why we are here. The question of whither we go, or whither they have gone, is still unanswered. But I think that Dan and Doris Kimball did know why they were here.

Robert Lowell

Robert Lowell, distinguished American poet, received Pulitzer Prizes for <u>Lord Weary's Castle</u> and <u>The Robert Lowell Dolphin</u>. His other books have in cluded <u>Life Studies</u>, <u>For the Union Dead</u>, <u>Notebook</u>, and <u>History</u>.

TO ROBERT LOWELL

Poet of purity and of parsimony
using one sense at a time, sparingly.
Salt bleaching white the whiteness of light,
straining the hemp, not nylon line,
scraping the wood to bare the silk grain.

Searching in attics and sheds,
of life, salvaging shards and scraps,
of truth, parts of dead poets,
pieces of gods.

Myopic, in storms, you cross
the bridge of the faulted rocks
double agent of doubt, smuggler of truth.

Poet Priest of the bitter sacrament
what is behind the door in man's house,
what is beneath the cross in God's house?
Look through your less dark glass,
daring as much for man as for God.

---

[117] W. B. Yeats, "King and No King," in *The Collected Poems of W. B. Yeats* (New York, 1956), p. 90.

Wayne Morse

Wayne Morse (1900 1974) began his career as a professor of law. He was elected to the United States Senate from Oregon in 1944 and served in the Senate for twenty four years. An early opponent of the Vietnam war, Senator Morse was also noted for his work on labor and education legislation.

I write from the experience of some thirty years during which I admired Wayne Morse: ten of those years before I had ever met him, some twenty years of companionship and common work in the Congress of the United States, and twenty years of friendship.

When I first ran for the United States Senate in 1958, I had been in the House of Representatives for ten years and had observed during that time the Senate and the men who were there - not just where they stood on issues but how they reflected in their judgments what the Senate should be. So when I ran, I asked two senators to come and campaign for me. One was Senator Paul Douglas, and the other was Senator Wayne Morse.

I will not write of Wayne's stand on the issues, for that is well known, but rather of his conception of and his respect for the Senate.

He was, of course, always the Senator from Oregon. But he was at the same time a United States Senator -- truly aware of the function of that body in the operation of this Republic. He knew that the Senate had a strong defensive responsibility: to stand against the House of Representatives, when that was necessary, and to lay down a challenge to the courts. And the second was a point which worried him a great deal. I thought of him in the summer of 1974 as we anticipated the Supreme Court decision on Watergate -- how Wayne Morse, along with great constitutional observers like Alexis de Tocqueville, had said that the ultimate test of democracy in this country might come through the courts. And, of course, he was concerned about the concentration of power in the executive.

In order to meet these responsibilities as he saw them, he rose whenever it was necessary above partisanship, even to the point of leaving the Republican party and of moving to the Democratic party. But in that party, too, he was always on the edge of defiance and challenge.

Wayne was never a member of "The Club," as they say in the Senate. This was not a matter of personality - because anyone who knew Wayne knew what a great companion he could be - but rather a matter of principle, because the Senate was never intended to be a club. I do not know whether he came to this position from reading Plato or by his own reasoning. But Plato, in talking about the Guardians of the State, said they should never become boon companions. And I have tried to follow Wayne's leadership and example in this respect.

He never succumbed to what C. S. Lewis called the temptation of the Inner Ring, which Lewis said is the temptation, the enticement, to accept the idea that you have joined a special group and, consequently, that you can act according to special rules. Lewis said that this temptation often leads very good men to do very bad things. Wayne was never tempted very much by that appeal.

His great concern was over the danger of power in our country - over power that was properly defined and properly used. But particularly he was concerned about it if it was secret power, if it was power which could not be called to explain itself or justify itself.

He showed this not only on great issues but also in little things that received scarcely any public attention. Back in 1959 we raised in the Senate the issue of the confirmation of a man named Lewis Strauss, who had been nominated to be the Secretary of Commerce. No one believes that the Secretaries of Commerce can do much harm. They just read the economic reports in the most optimistic tone every two or three weeks and go back to their offices. But there were two things involved in the Strauss case. Lewis Strauss had said, in another office, that he did not think the executive branch had to carry out the laws as Congress had drafted and approved them. He also said that he really did not think the executive agencies had to tell Congress what Congress thought it had to know in order to legislate. So despite the relatively unimportant office at stake, two vital constitutional questions were raised. And Wayne felt they had to be raised and pursued.

Shortly after the election of President Kennedy, at a caucus of Democratic senators, it was proposed that the

Vice President be allowed to preside over the caucuses. There was not much involved there, because we really did not hold any caucuses. But it was a question of principle. And Wayne, as I recall, made an argument from the history of the British Parliament, in which he said that the agents of the King were not allowed to sit in parliamentary conferences. So following him and with some help from others, we had seventeen votes against having the Vice President preside over the caucuses. It was a question of principle. It was a matter of drawing the line, of saying, "You meet your responsibility, and we will meet ours."

In that same spirit, of course, he moved to oppose the war in Vietnam. I remember what, I think, was the first significant meeting in opposition, when the Clergy and Laymen Concerned About Vietnam came to Washington early in 1967. Wayne spoke and said the war was illegal. Senator Ernest Gruening of Alaska spoke - the voice of a prophet - and said it was immoral. I was the third speaker and, since the legality had been taken care of and also the morality, there was not much left for me to talk about. So I said I thought it was a foolish war. Together we thought we had made the total and complete case against the war. We proceeded from that point through many difficult years to give the country the opportunity to make a moral judgment about the war, and to try to induce its political leaders to change attitudes and habits and practices along the way.

That is the general public record. But I would like to speak of some more personal things again, the question of integrity in small things. (It is not difficult for us to show integrity in great national forums.) Wayne would never simply extend his remarks in the Congressional Record. Many senators, especially late in the afternoon when there is no audience, speak for a few minutes and then put the rest of the speech in the Record, and it appears as though they had given it. But Wayne would never do that. You could go over to the Senate sometimes at five or six o'clock in the afternoon and hear him speak for an hour. Sometimes there were only two or three people in the galleries, sometimes only his wife. But I often thought of how many people over the years who were there late in the afternoon were impressed to hear Senator Morse telling them and telling the country what he thought it should hear - and never making the rather easy compromise, which nearly everyone else in the Senate made, of simply saying, "Well, I will put it in the Record and get it printed and then distribute it the next day."

He served well, also, by way of relieving tension on the floor of the Senate. One of his practices was to keep a box of licorice in his desk. He would reward people; I think it was the old schoolmaster in him. He would say, "You have done well today; you can come down and have a piece of licorice." It got to be rather a mark of prestige if you were approved - and especially if you were allowed free access to the licorice box. It was more or less the ultimate test if you did not have to ask permission. He would occasionally demand that you replenish the supply, but even that was an indication that he had somehow approved you and accepted you as a person deserving of full trust and confidence.

Wayne talked a great deal about cattle, and I visited his farm many times. He had, among the red and blue ribbons, many lavender ones, which I had not seen much of. I asked, "What are those?" He said, "Well, that is the ribbon for best of breed." Of course, he raised Devon cattle, and I accused him of having the only Devon entry in all the fairs, so that he was almost certain to win the ribbon for best of breed. He denied that, and he and I became defenders of Devon cattle over the years.

I would note that the greatest testimony to him was that as he grew older, the confidence and trust of the young people in him grew in strength and intensity. I can think of no higher tribute than that. Of course, his belief in the younger people - and particularly as he talked about his grandchildren - grew with that same strength. It was reciprocal trust.

Let me conclude with some lines from a poem written by a Welshman named Vernon Watkins. The title is "*A True Picture Restored*," the subtitle, "*Memories of Dylan Thomas*." The poem was written soon after the death of Thomas, and it contains these lines which I think apply to Wayne Morse:

The latest dead, the latest dead,
How should he have died...

And Wales, when shall you have again
One so true as he,
Whose hand was on the mountain's heart,

The rising of the sea,
And every praising bird that cries
Above the estuary?...

"My immortality," he said,
"Now matters to my soul
Less than the deaths of others."...

Let each whose soul is in one place
Still to that place be true.
The man I mourn could honour such
With every breath he drew.
I never heard him wish to take
A life from where it grew.

And yet the man I mourn is gone,
He who could give the rest
So much to live for till the grave,
And do it all in jest.
Hard it must be, beyond this day,
For even the grass to rest.[118]

---

[118] Vernon Watkins, "A True Picture Restored," <u>Selected Poems, 1930-1960</u> (London, 1967), pp. 72-76.

Lewis Mumford

Lewis Mumford, social philosopher and critic, has taught at several universities. He is a leading authority on the city and the author of many books, including The Myth of the Machine and The Urban Prospect.

Lewis Mumford's efforts to draw the attention of the country to the reality of urbanization and to the need for rational ordering of city life have distinguished him through the years. If one were to make a list of great books which, had sufficient attention been paid, would have changed the culture of the United States and would have prevented degradation and disorder, the books of Lewis Mumford would have to be listed among the most significant.

After the first or second moon landing, I thought that the subsequent flights should have been directed to places like East St. Louis and Newark. The astronauts sent to those places could have been instructed to bring back eighty to one hundred pounds of material. Upon analysis the material brought back would have indicated that there had once been cities on the sites visited, with a culture somewhere between the Late Iron and the Early Plastic ages, but that the sites no longer supported human life.

Not only has Lewis Mumford written about a most important subject in warning of this trend but he has written books under siege. The need for books was challenged first by magazines using the written word and then by magazines using pictures. But Life, the original picture news magazine of our time, finally was done in by its own methodology - by color television with its instant history and multiple choices. Now I fear that the English language may disappear some Sunday afternoon between the opening of *Face the Nation* and the end of *Issues and Answers* if it survives *Meet the Press*. After the collapse there will be nothing left but an assortment of adjectives with a few adverbs thrown in.

We honor Lewis Mumford not only because he has written about important subjects, and written about them in books, but also because he has written well. He has honored and respected the English language. He has written in the context of history and in the context of ideas. He has insisted that good judgment and reason can give direction to history and can improve the quality of American cities and American life.

Eleanor Roosevelt

Eleanor Roosevelt (1884-1962) was a principal adviser to her husband, Franklin D. Roosevelt throughout his political career. Mrs. Roosevelt was also a columnist and the author of many books.

Eleanor Roosevelt entered the marketplace of action and controversy. She was more than a commentator. Her accepted role was not to judge the world, but to save and improve it. She had the qualities of tolerance and forgiveness, for she knew the capacity of men for confusion and misunderstanding.

She never allowed her interest in humanity to distract her from interest in men and women or from service to persons.

Although she believed that the movement of history was toward a better life, she never allowed hopes or dreams of a better future to interfere with dedicated action and attention to the present. Tomorrow Is Now was the title of her last book.

Eleanor Roosevelt was a realist, ready to accept compromise but only when principle was recognized and given the greater weight on the scales. She was prepared - when she could not be sure - to make mistakes on the side of trust rather than on the side of mistrust and suspicion, to make mistakes on the side of liberality and hope rather an on the side of narrow self-concern and fear.

She was blessed, as were all who knew her, in that as she grew in age, she also grew in spiritual strength and wisdom.

In her political life and in the days when truth was being driven from the field, when doubt was expanded, when suspicion and accusation held the high ground, when younger persons fled in fear, Eleanor Roosevelt stood firm.

One writer described her as "fine, precise, hand-worked like ivory."[119] And she became, like a figure carved in ivory, more beautiful with age.

---

[119] Norman Mailer, "Superman Comes to the Supermart," *Esquire*, November 1960, p. 121.

She reached that high state of serenity in which she moved and spoke and acted freely, without fear and without concern for the judgment of biographers or any judgment of the world.

Frank Rosenblatt

Frank Rosenblatt (1928-1971) was a research scientist and a teacher. He was most active in work for peace. Dr. Rosenblatt was also a leader in the Cornell University community and a great friend to his students. He died in a boating accident on his forty-third birthday.

In paying tribute to Frank Rosenblatt, I could say little from any direct personal knowledge of what he did. I write of him principally in what I know of his influence on other people.

As I tried to define his character, I concluded that it was angelic. Not angelic according to that view of angels in which they are seen as vague and uncommitted beings, but to another in which they are as beings of absolute moral and intellectual commitment.

Frank spent little time passing moral judgment on other people. He acted like someone who had decided that he would do what he could to eliminate the evil and distress that arise from ignorance and false knowledge, and leave the passing of moral judgments to others. Following that decision, his commitment was complete.

Frank was a brother to the members of his family, to the members of the faculty at Cornell, to the students, to the land, to all things of creation. Even in his death he left no person to carry blame. He died by things he loved and left them unblamed - the unseen wind and the waiting sea.

Adlai Stevenson

Adlai E. Stevenson 11 (1900-1965) served as Governor of Illinois, Democratic presidential candidate in 1952 and 1956, and United States Ambassador to the United Nations.

When I nominated him to be the Democratic presidential candidate in 1960, the United States economy was in a recession. There was great tension between the United States and Russia and also between the United States and Cuba. A civil war had just broken out in the Congo. Following is the nomination speech, which was given on July 13, 1960, in Los Angeles, California.

Mr. Chairman, Democratic delegates at this great convention:

We now approach the hour of all important decision. You are the chosen people out of one hundred and seventy two million Americans, the chosen of the Democratic party, come here to Los Angeles not only to choose a man to lead this Democratic party in the campaign of this fall and this November but to choose a man who we hope will lead this country and all of our friends and all of those peoples who look to us for help, who look to us for understanding, who look to us for leadership.

We are here participating in the great test of democratic society. As you know, our way of life is being challenged today. There are those, the enemies of democracy, who say that free men and free women cannot exercise that measure of intellectual responsibility, cannot demonstrate that measure of moral responsibility, which is called for to make the kind of decisions that we free people are called upon to make in this year of 1960. And there are those, I remind you, who are the friends of democracy, who have expressed some doubt and some reserve as to whether or not this ideology, this way of life, these institutions of ours, can survive.

Let me ask you at this time to put aside all of your prejudices, to put aside any kind of unwarranted regional loyalties, to put aside for the time being preferences which are based purely upon questions of personality. Put aside, if you can, early decisions - decisions which were made before all of the candidates were in the race, decisions which were made at another season of the year, decisions which were made when the issues were not clear, as they are today.

I say to those of you - candidates and spokesmen for candidates - who say you are confident of the strength that you have at this convention, who say that you are confident and believe in democracy - let this go to a second ballot.

I say let this go to a second ballot, when every delegate who is here will be as free as he can be free to make a decision.

Let us strike off the fetters of instructed delegations. Let governors say to their people, "This is the moment of decision and we want you to make it as free Americans, responsible to your own conscience and to the people of the state that sent you here, and to the people of this country."

This I say is the real test of democracy. Do you have confidence .in the people at this convention to make a fair and responsible choice, or do you not have that confidence?

What has happened in this world and what has happened in this United States has been described to you here by great speakers. Each new headline every day that we have been here has been a shock to us.

These times, people say, are out of joint. They say these are the worst of times without being the best of times - this may be true. But I say to you these external signs, these practical problems which face us are nothing compared to the problems of the mind and of the spirit which face the United States and the free world today.

If the mind is clouded and if the will is confused and uncertain, there can be no sound decision and no sound action.

There is demagoguery abroad in the land at all times, and demagoguery, I say to you, takes many forms. There is that which says, "here is wealth, and here is material comfort." We suffer a little from that in the United States.

There is demagoguery which promises people power, which is used for improper purposes and ends. And we have seen in this century and in this generation what happens when power is abused.

I say to you there is a subtle kind of demagoguery which erodes the will, which erodes the spirit. And this is the demagoguery which has affected this United States in the last eight years.

What are we told? What have we been told? We have been told that we can be strong without sacrifice. This is what we have been told. We have been told that we can be good without any kind of discipline if we just say we are humble and sincere - this is the nature of goodness. We have been told that we can be wise without reflection. We can be wise without study, we have been told. I say this is the erosion of the spirit which has taken place in this United States in the last eight years.

And I say to you that the time has come to raise again the cry of the ancient prophet. What did he say? He said the prophets prophesy falsely; and the high priests, he said, rule by their word, and my people love to have it so. But what will be the end thereof?

I say to you the political prophets have prophesied falsely in these eight years. And the high priests of government have ruled by that false prophecy. And the people seemed to have loved it so.

But there was one man - there was one man who did not prophesy falsely, let me remind you. There was one man who said, "Let's talk sense to the American people."[120]

What did the scoffers say? The scoffers said, "Nonsense." They said, "Catastrophic nonsense." But we know it was the essential and the basic and the fundamental truth that he spoke to us. This was the man who talked sense to the American people.

There was one man who said: This is a time for self-examination. This is a time for us to take stock, he said. This is a time to decide where we are and where we are going.

This, he said, is a time for virtue. But what virtues did he say we needed? Oh, yes, he said, we need the heroic virtues - we always do. We need fortitude; we need courage; we need justice. Everyone cheers when you speak out for those virtues.

But what did he say in addition to that? He said we need the unheroic virtues in America. We need the virtue,

---

[120] Adlai Ewing Stevenson, *The Stark Reality of Responsibility* (Chicago, 1952), p. 19, speech accepting the Democratic presidential nomination, July 26, 1952.

he said, of patience. There were those who said we have had too much of patience.

We need, he said, the virtue of tolerance. We need the virtue of forbearance. We need the virtue of patient understanding.

This was what the prophet said. This is what he said to the American people. I ask you, did he prophesy falsely? Did he prophesy falsely?

He said this is a time for greatness. This is a time for greatness for America. He did not say he possessed it. He did not even say he was destined for it. He did say that the heritage of America is one of greatness.

And he described that heritage to us. And he said the promise of America is a promise of greatness. And he said this promise we must fulfill.

This was his call to greatness. This was the call to greatness that was as issued in 1952.

He did not seek power for himself in 1952. He did not seek power in 1956.

He does not seek it for himself today.

This man knows, as all of us do from history, that power often comes to those who seek it. But history does not prove that power is always well used by those who seek it.

On the contrary, the whole history of democratic politics is to this end: that power is best exercised by those who are sought out by the people, by those to whom power is given by a free people.

And so I say to you Democrats here assembled: Do not turn away from this man. Do not reject this man. He has fought gallantly. He has fought courageously. He has fought honorably. In 1952 in the great battle. In 1956 he fought bravely. And between those years and since, he has stood off the guerrilla attacks of his enemies and the sniping attacks of those who should have been his friends.

Do not reject this man who made us all proud to be called Democrats. Do not reject this man who, his enemies said, spoke, above the heads of the people, but they said it only because they did not want the people to listen. He spoke to the people. He moved their minds and stirred their hearts, and this was what was objected to. Do not leave this prophet without honor in his own party. Do not reject this man.

I submit to you a man who is not the favorite son of any one state. I submit to you the man who is the favorite son of fifty states.

And not only of fifty states, but the favorite son of every country in the world in which he is known -- the favorite son in every country in which he is unknown but in which some spark, even though unexpressed, of desire for liberty and freedom still lives.

This favorite son I submit to you: Adlai Stevenson of Illinois.

* * *

When Adlai Stevenson died, we lost the purest politician of our time.

Stevenson's approach to politics was marked by three principal characteristics:

First, a decent respect to the opinions of mankind in world affairs.

Second, a willingness to accept the judgment of the majority in domestic politics and in general elections.

Third, the unselfish surrender of his own personal reputation and image for the good of the common effort if, in his judgment, that surrender would advance the cause of justice and order and civility. Adlai Stevenson did not grow in honor and in reputation through the organizations which he served, but rather they grew by virtue of his service.

He demonstrated early in his career and throughout his public life the highest degree of political humility in his indifference to what historians and biographers might say about him.

Stevenson was not ahead of his times or outside of his times, as some of his critics said. He was a true contemporary, passing judgment on his own day, expressing that judgment in words that proved his deep concern for the integrity of the language, and finally committing himself to the consequences of his judgment.

In the words of Chaucer, he was a worthy knight who from the time he first rode forth "loved chivalry, truth and honor, generosity and courtesy."[121]

---

[121] Geoffrey Chaucer, The Canterbury Tales, trans. by Vincent F. Hopper (Woodbury, N.Y., 1970), p. 4.

Sources

Acheson, Dean Present at the Creation (New York, 1969)

Adams, John Diary and Autobiography of John Adams, ed. by L. H. Butterfield (Cambridge, Mass., 1961)

Adams, John Letters of John Adams Addressed to His Wife, ed. by Charles Francis Adams (Boston, 1841)

Adams, John The Works of John Adams, ed. by Charles Francis Adams (Boston, 1856)

Benton, Walter from Never a Greater Need, (1948 Knopf)

Berrigan, Daniel S.J., No Bars to Manhood (New York, 1971)

Bich, Nguyen Ngoc, ed. A Thousand Years of Vietnamese Poetry, (New York,1975)

Bolt, Robert A Man for All Seasons (New York, 1962)

Burke, Edmund Reflections on the Revolution in France (Los Angeles, 1955)

Bynner, Witter from Book of Lyrics (1955 by Witter Bynner)

Chaucer, Geoffrey The Canterbury Tales

Chesterton, G. K. What I Saw in America (London, 1922)

Churchill, Winston S. Blood, Sweat, and Tears (New York, 1941)

Cromie, Robert, ed., Where Steel Winds Blow (New York, 1968)

Cromwell, Oliver The Writings and Speeches of Oliver Cromwell, ed. by William Cortez Abbott (New York, 1970)

Dunne, Finley P. Dissertations by Mr. Dooley (New York, 1906)

Federalist Papers, No. 68. Alexander Hamilton, James Madison, and John Jay

Frankfurter, Felix dissenting opinion in Lee v. United States, in United States Reports (Washington, 1952)

Fromm, Erich The Revolution of Hope (New York, 1968)

Gallienne, Richard Le "The Illusion of War" from New Poems Dodd, Mead

Gallienne, Richard Le "The Illusion of War," in Vincent Godfrey Burns, ed., The Red Harvest (New York, 1930)

Gordon, George Lord Byron, Don Juan

Gide, André The Journals of André Gide, trans. by Justin O'Brien (New York, 1951)

Hersh, Seymour H. My Lai 4 (New York, 1970)

Jefferson, Thomas The Writings of Thomas Jefferson, ed. by
Andrew A. Lipscomb (Washington, 1903)

Lewis, C. S., "The Inner Ring," in Transposition and Other
Addresses (London, 1949)

Lowell, Robert from Land of Unlikeness, (1944, Farrar,
Straus & Giroux)

Mailer, Norman "Superman Comes to the Supermart,"
Esquire, November 1960

More, Thomas The Utopia of Sir Thomas More, ed. by
Mildred Campbell (New York, 1947)

Nixon, Richard M. "The Second Choice," in The 1964 World
Book Year Book (Chicago, 1964)

Orwell, George "Politics and English Language," in A
Collection of Essays (New York, 1954)

Parkinson, Northcote Parkinson's Law (Boston, 1957)

Po, Li "The Long War" from War and the Poet,
Eberhart/Rodman (1945 Devin-Adair Co.)

Public Papers of the Presidents: Dwight D. Eisenhower,
1960-61 (Washington, 1961)

Public Papers of the Presidents: John F. Kennedy, 1963
(Washington, 1964)

Public Papers of the Presidents: Harry S. Truman, 1948
(Washington, 1964)

Public Papers of the Presidents: Richard Nixon, 1971
(Washington, 1972)

Reedy, George E. The Twilight of the Presidency (New York
and Cleveland, 1970)

Sandburg, Carl, from "Grass" from Complete Poems of Carl
Sandburg. Harcourt Brace Jovanovich

Sassoon, Siegfried "'They'" from Collected Poems Viking
Press

Seferis, George Poems, trans. by Rex Warner (London,1960)

Shakespeare, William Measure for Measure,

Shirer, William L. The Rise and Fall of the Third Reich
(New York, 1960)

Stafford, William "Connections," in West of Your City (Los
Gatos, Calif., 1960)

Tocqueville, Alexis de Democracy in America, ed. by J. P.
Mayer (Garden City, N.Y., 1969)

Tuong,Tu Ke "That Painter in the City" (1967 by Asia
Society, Inc.) from A Thousand Years of Vietnamese
Poetry, edited by Nguyen Ngoc Bich, translated by Nguyen
Ngoc Bich with Burton Raffel and W. S. Merwin.

Vizinczey, Stephen The Rules of Chaos (New York, 1969)

Warren, Thomas Herbert Poetry and War (London 1915)

Watkins, Vernon "A True Picture Restored: Memories of Dylan Thomas,", Selected Poems, (1967 Faber & Faber)
Webster, Daniel The Writings and Speeches of Daniel Webster, ed. by Fletcher Webster (Boston, 1903)
White, William S. The Citadel (New York, 1957)
Whittier, John Greenleaf "Barbara Frietchie," in The Patriotic Anthology (New York, 1941)
Wirt, William Sketches of the Life and Character of Patrick Henry (Philadelphia, 1817)
Yeats, William Butler "On Being Asked for a War Poem" from Collected Poems (1919 Macmillan)
Zola, Émile La Vérité en Marche (Paris, 1901)

Index

B

B-1 bomber, 67
Baker, Howard, 57
Ball, George, 104
Barbara Frietchie, 136
Barkley, Alben, 35
Barnburners, 91
Bartlett, E. L., 38
*Battle Hymn of the
Republic*, 136
Bay of Pigs, 23, 62, 69
Bayh, Birch, 43
Becket, Thomas A, 173
Benevolent incapacitators,
129
Bennett, John, 177
Benton, Walter, 133, 136
Berrigan, Daniel, 46, 106
Berrigan, Philip, 46
Bill of Rights, 45, 176
Bly, Robert, 138
Bolt, Robert, 105
Bomber, The, 135
Bowering, George, 138
brain trust, 102
Brown, Jerry, 123
Brown, Sam, 123
Bryan, William Jennings,
36
Buchanan, James, 91
Buckley, William F. Jr., 166
Bundy, McGeorge, 102
Bunker, Ellsworth, 63
Burger, Warren, 43, 46
Burke, Edmund, 153
Burning the News, 138
Burning Tree Country
Club, 51
Burrow, The, 70
Bynner, Witter, 135

C

Cambodia, 41, 60, 62, 128,
175
Cambodia, invasion, 120
Camp David, 27
Carswell, G. Harrold, 42
Case, Clifford, 42
Cass, Lewis, 91
cattle, Devon, 189
Caulfield, John, 52, 53
censorship, 174
Central Intelligence
Agency, 14, 39, 41, 56,
69
   actions with executive
      approval usually the
      problem, 70
   methods and
      instruments, 70
Channing, Carol as an
   enemy of the state, 167
Chesterton, G. K., 102,
144, 156
Chile, 69, 72
Church, Frank, 42
Churchill, Winston, 127
Citadel, The, 37
Clarke, Austin, 138, 140
Clausewitz, 60
Clergy and Laymen
   Concerned About
   Vietnam, 188
Clifford, Clark, 106
Coffin, William Sloane Jr.,
173
Colby, William, 57
Colson, Charles, 166
Columbus, 145
Commager, Henry Steele,
49
Committee for the Re-
election of the President,
171
Common Cause, 112, 169

J

Jackson State College, 122, 165
Jackson, Andrew, 90
Jarrell, Randall, 138
jaw-boning sessions, 74
Jefferson, Thomas, 35, 151
John Brown's Body, 136
Johnson, Lyndon, 8, 10, 11, 12, 13, 14, 21, 25, 33, 39, 84, 96, 101, 107
Jones, James, 138
judge the political systems of other nations, 13
justifications, specious
   if we don't, they will, 64

K

Kafka, Franz, 70, 118
Kaiser Bill, 137
Kefauver, Estes, 96
Kellogg-Briand Pact, 58
Kennedy, John, 10, 14, 21, 84, 86, 95, 101, 102, 122, 180, 181, 182
Kennedy, Robert, 8, 9, 96
Kent State University, 120, 122
Keynes
   we are beyond, 147
Keynesian, 84, 146
Keynesian, post-post, 154
Khe Sanh, 64
Kimball, Dan, 183
Kimball, Doris Fleeson, 183
King, Martin Luther Jr., 165
Kissinger, Henry, 29, 46, 101, 102
Kittredge, Walter, 136
Kleindienst, Richard, 51

Know-Nothings, 91, 92
Korean War, 74
Krupp, 170

L

La Follette, Robert M. Sr., 92
Laird, Melvin, 129
language of politics, 127
Laos, 60, 62, 69, 171
Lawrence, Fr Emeric, 179
lawyers as U.S.Supreme Court justices
   arguments against, 47
Lekachman, Robert, 154
Lewis, C. S., 71, 172, 187
Liddy, G. Gordon, 51
Lincoln Memorial, 120
Lincoln, Abraham, 21, 91
lobbyist, 111
Lockheed, 19, 74, 109
Lowell, Robert, 135, 137, 185

M

MacArthur, Douglas, 29, 105
Mademoiselle from Armentières, 137
Magruder, Jeb Stuart, 173
Mailer, Norman, 119, 138
man as subject of history rather than object, 149
manned-bomber program
   greatest public-works project in the history of the United States, if not of mankind, 67
Mansfield, Mike, 98
Marching through Georgia, 136
Maritain, Jacques, 147, 179
Marshall, Alfred, 154

206

Marxism, 82
Marxists, 170
Maryland, My Maryland, 136
mass communication can pervert as well as educate, 80
Mathias, Charles, 42
May Day march of 1971 10,000 arrested, 121
May Day protest, 1971, 120
McCarthy, Joseph, 39
McCloskey, Paul, 98
McCord, James, 57, 172
McGee, Gale, 38
McGovern Movement, 126
McGovern, George, 8, 84, 85, 87, 88, 95
McNamara, Robert, 25, 64, 106, 118, 119, 180
Measure for Measure, 173
Mexican connection, 56
Michener, James, 138
militarization of foreign policy, 62
military action in a policy vacuum is like clergy trying to operate without theology, 59
military influence on education, 68
military involvement in domestic affairs, 66
military language has invaded civilian politics, 82
military role inversion, 60
military-industrial complex, 22, 61
military-industrial-academic establishment, 61
Millikin, Eugene, 38
Minnesota Mining, 171

mislabeling, dangers, 58
Mississippi Freedom Democratic party, 90
Mitchell, John, 54, 164
Mobilization Committee to End the War in Vietnam, 119
More, Sir Thomas, 20, 105, 126
Morgenthau, Hans J., 166
Morse, Wayne, 186
Moses, 93
Moss, Frank, 38
Moyers, Bill, 105
Mumford, Lewis, 191
Murder in the Cathedral, 173
Muskie, Edmund, 38, 97
My Lai 4, 130, 165
Myth of the Machine, The, 191

N

Nader, Ralph, 18, 112
Namath, Joe as an enemy of the state, 167
National Association of Manufacturers, 115
National Democratic party of Alabama, 90
National Farmers Union, 113
national health insurance, 76
National Industrial Recovery Act, 28
National Student Association, 55
National Urban League, 55
National Welfare Rights Organization, 55
NATO, 64
Navajo Tribe, 112
Nazism, 169

About the Author

Eugene J. McCarthy was born in Watkins, Minnesota, in 1916, graduated from St. John's University in Collegeville, Minnesota, in 1935, and received a Master of Arts from the University of Minnesota in 1938.

During World War II, he served as a civilian technical assistant in military intelligence for the War Department. He was acting head of the sociology department at the College of St. Thomas in St. Paul at the time of his election to Congress in 1948.

Re-elected four more times, Mr. McCarthy represented Minnesota's 4th District in the House of Representatives for ten years, serving on Post Office & Civil Service, Agriculture, Interior & Insular Affairs, Banking & Currency, and Ways & Means committees.

McCarthy served two terms in the U.S. Senate from 1959 to 1971, serving on the Finance, Agriculture & Forestry, and Public Works committees, the Senate Special Committee on Unemployment Problems and from 1965 to 1969 he served on the Senate Foreign Relations Committee and chaired the special subcommittee on African Affairs. His run for the presidency in 1968, reported in this book, electrified the nation and forced a national political debate on issues fundamental to the operation of a deomocratic state. In 1976 and 1992 McCarthy again ran for the presidency to bring forward some discussion of these fundamentals, examined herein and in many of his other books which include:

America Revisited (Doubleday)
An American Bestiary (Lone Oak Press)
And Time Began (Lone Oak Press)
Challenge of Freedom (Avon)
Colony of the World (Hippocrene)
Complexities & Contraries (Harcourt)
Dictionary of American Politics (Macmillan)
Frontiers in American Democracy (World Publishing)
Ground Fog & Night (Harcourt)

Liberal Answer to the Conservative Challenge
(Macfadden-Bartell)
Limits of Power (Holt)
Memories of a Native Son (Lone Oak Press)
Mr. Raccoon & His Friends (Academy Chicago)
No-Fault Politics (Times Books)
Nonfinancial Economic (Praeger)
Required Reading (Harcourt)
Selected Poems (Lone Oak Press)
Ultimate Tyranny (Harcourt)
Up 'Til Now (Harcourt)
View From Rappahannock (Lone Oak Press)